FOR THE LOVE OF MOOSE

How one man's trash became my treasure.

Margaret Lee

For The Love Of Moose Creations

Copyright © 2023 Margaret Lee

All rights reserved

The characters and events portrayed in this book are fictitious. Any similarity to real persons, living or dead, is coincidental and not intended by the author.

No part of this book may be reproduced, or stored in a retrieval system, or transmitted in any form or by any means, electronic, mechanical, photocopying, recording, or otherwise, without express written permission of the publisher.

ISBN: 9798385547944

Cover design by: Art Painter
Library of Congress Control Number: 2018675309
Printed in the United States of America

To the ones who speak volumes without uttering a word, the ones who suffer yet forgive time and time again, the ones who never lose hope the ones who fight the good fight because their hearts and souls would have it no other way— and especially to those who love without condition, be they human or canine.

All his life he tried to be a good person. Many times, however, he failed. For after all, he was only human. He wasn't a dog.

—CHARLES M. SCHULZ

CONTENTS

Title Page
Copyright
Dedication
Epigraph
Foreword
Preface
For The Love of moose

Chapter 1	1
Chapter 2	13
Chapter 3	18
Chapter 4	22
Chapter 5	27
Chapter 6	32
Chapter 7	36
Chapter 8	40
Chapter 9	44
Chapter 10	51
Chapter 11	58
Chapter 12	62
Chapter 13	68
Chapter 14	73

Chapter 15	80
Chapter 16	86
Chapter 17	96
Chapter 18	107
Chapter 19	111
Chapter 20	116
Chapter 21	124
Chapter 22	129
Chapter 23	136
Afterword	141
About The Author	143
for the love of moose	145

FOREWORD

My path crossed Margaret's in the summer of 2011. Our correspondence started with an e-mail she sent to me stating she was looking for a trainer to assist her with training her dogs. Helping dog owners is how I make a living. I've spent thousands of hours working with dog owners with all types of dog problems. Margaret's e-mail, however, piqued my interest more than most. She stated that she had five dogs and was experiencing some aggressive behavior within her pack. My wife and I had five dogs also and knew very well how challenging it can be to manage a group of dogs of that size. I was looking forward to meeting Margaret and finding out more about her dogs and how she came across them.

As we began our lessons, I was surprised how much Margaret knew about her dogs individually. She was the type of client who never complained about her dogs' behavior to me. Rather, she was curious about how she could improve her communication with them. Margaret's dogs were not bad dogs. They were just dogs.

Today we find ourselves inundated with the idea that if your dog doesn't have the ability to get along with all people, all other dogs, and all other animals, the owner is to blame for not raising their dog the right way. In reality, dogs were never designed to fill all of those roles.

In this book, Margaret gives dog owners a refreshing

glimpse at what it's like to bring a challenging dog into your life. She gives us insight into how to persist through moments of feeling like a failure. Each of her five dogs comes with its own story, and most of them didn't have a good start in life. Margaret's journey with her dogs weaves through the emotional baggage from previous owners, cruises through the proud moments, and then reminds us that dead ends are possible at every turn.

In this beautifully written book, Margaret details the highs and lows of living with dogs in a way that I have not seen in any other text. She explores the wide range of emotions that we feel when we share our lives with dogs throughout our ever-changing lives. This isn't a fairy tale about a dog that turns out to be a hero. This is a book about what real dogs can teach us when we learn how to begin truly seeing our dogs and accepting them for who they are as individuals.

Tommy Grammer, CPDT-KA
Professional dog trainer
Evergreen School For Dogs

PREFACE

As a child, I wasn't allowed to have a dog for a pet. My parents let me have cats, and I had a few, but it was my dream to one day have a dog. When I purchased my own home many years later, I decided it was time to fulfill that dream.

At the time, I knew of no other place than the local animal shelter to search for my first dog. The breed of dog was not an issue. I had no problem going to the shelter and picking out a homeless mixed-breed dog. But I did have some preconceived notions about dogs. Large, powerful dogs drew my attention, even though they scared me. I was ignorant and easily persuaded when it came to these breeds. Dramatic news stories pulled me in and tainted my belief system.

Historically, the media has focused negative attention on German shepherds, Rottweilers, pit bulls, and Dobermans. I had encountered German shepherds, Rottweilers, and Dobermans and found them to be gentle giants. The media did manage to convince me pit bulls are dangerous and unpredictable. I didn't have many opportunities to meet pit bulls, so I believed the hype surrounding that breed for many years.

My search led me to a German shepherd that became my perfect first dog. He was ten years old, and his previous owner had taken the time to teach him basic commands. He was well mannered, easygoing, and didn't cause any problems. After he passed, I adopted four more dogs, all mixed breeds, all rescues.

These four all lived together and were a diverse pack. Their cohesiveness took many years of training, patience, tears, and hard work.

The fifth and last dog I brought into this mix was Moose. I found Moose when he was a puppy, about three months old. When someone later told me Moose might be a pit bull, I panicked. I didn't think I had what it took to handle such a powerful and potentially unstable dog.

What I didn't foresee was that this tiny puppy was going to change who I was. A catalyst is a substance that affects change without itself being changed or consumed. One catalyst molecule can transform several million reactant molecules. Moose was my catalyst. He would dispel the media's poisons, teaching me about powerful dogs and my ability to handle them.

Moose has an all-encompassing dislike for animals. Dogs, cats, horses, and cows all make his list, which made managing his personality a challenge. This trait isn't exclusive to any breed. Some dogs don't care for small children, and some dogs don't like people other than their owner. I was lucky; Moose adored all human beings.

Substances that reduce the effectiveness of a catalyst are called catalyst inhibitors or catalyst poisons. I encountered many poisons along the way. I needed help managing this powerful animal, so I searched for a trainer. One trainer I contacted told me I should put Moose down because he was part pit bull; I had encountered my first catalyst poison. When I tried to relocate Moose in a working field as a bomb dog, I discovered poisons there too. Ironically, I later learned Moose didn't even have pit bull blood.

When I finally found a talented trainer, my miracle worker, the catalyst went to work and changed my beliefs evermore. Moose responded well to training and was a fast learner. He was a superstar and lived to please. I learned a bit slower, but I learned. A good dog trainer is a great people trainer as well.

You never know what you're going to get when you rescue

a dog. Each dog has the potential to teach you something about yourself—some of it good and some of it you wish would have stayed hidden. Moose showed me both and then changed me for the better. I didn't change him; I learned to manage him. He changed my perceptions through love and patience. It was a surprise to me how much work I needed.

Dogs, like humans, are individuals with quirks, shortcomings, tempers, and preferences. Where they differ from humans is their ability to suffer at the hands of humans but still forgive and love those who slight them. Unconditional love will be my final hurdle. Maybe then I can be the person my dogs see in me.

FOR THE LOVE OF MOOSE

CHAPTER 1

Snickers

I've heard it said that once in your lifetime, you will find that irreplaceable dog, the one that is your soul mate. This is a story about my once-in-a-lifetime dog, Moose. Moose taught me about friendship, fear, love, patience, heartbreak, devotion, and so much more.

This story must begin by explaining how I fell in love with dogs. As mentioned earlier, I didn't have a dog growing up. I had cats, but those cats always had short lives, succumbing to various hazards. Some met tragic deaths, while others just disappeared. My mother didn't let me have a dog because she once had a German shepherd that died of cancer—and took her heart with him. She couldn't bear to lose another dog. Little did I know, history was bound to repeat itself.

After I graduated from college, I moved from Texas to Washington to start a life on my own. I was an apartment dweller for many years. Apartment owners don't like renters with pets unless they pay a large deposit. And a deposit is justifiable; pets can do much damage to a home.

I adopted the first cat of my adulthood, Smokey, when my neighbor moved. He transferred his deposit to my apartment on the condition that I take his cat. My cat parenting began again. She was a round-bellied, gray tabby cat with a sweet, petite face.

I felt Smokey was too masculine of a name, so I changed it to Miss Piggy. She took some warming up to, but she soon loved living with me in my six-hundred-square-foot apartment.

A couple of years later, a neighbor had two sister cats that became pregnant two weeks apart. I took one kitten from each of the two litters. The first cat my neighbor gave me was the runt of the firstborn litter. She was a domestic shorthaired cat, mostly white with black patches and tabby markings in the patches. I named her Sugar. Sugar was unpredictable; she would often strike out.

I chose a black cat from the second litter, which were born on Friday the thirteenth. My neighbor decided to give that cat to someone else and then showed me the kitten he'd picked out for me. This one was a tortoise-shelled tabby with the sweetest, prettiest face I'd ever seen. He thought she looked like Yoda from *Star Wars*, and I had to agree. I took her and named her Harleigh Ann. Her face and personality were a match. She was a sweet cat and always a favorite with visitors. These cats fared much better than the ones back home and lived their full life spans.

In my thirties, I decided it was time for a major lifestyle and career change. When I graduated from college in Texas, I had wanted to become a police officer, but my father forbade it. Looking back, I'm glad I didn't choose that career at that point in my life. I'm sure I would have failed, since I lacked life experience. Both my family and the city I grew up in were volatile, which was part of the reason I decided to leave once and for all.

I moved to the Pacific Northwest, and for ten years I managed businesses, mostly retail. The pay wasn't good, and I didn't feel I was realizing my potential. Once again, I explored a career in law enforcement, and this time decided to pursue it. I was quickly hired by a small city not far from where I was living. The work suited me, and I was fully on track for adulthood.

I set new goals for myself. At the top of my list was buying a house. The housing market in Washington was booming, and I thought I'd never be able to afford one on my own. The second thing on my list was to fulfill my lifelong dream of having a dog. I found a house at a reasonable price in a new development. It was small on a small lot in a now densely populated neighborhood. It was affordable, and it was soon mine.

So much work needs to be done to a house in a new neighborhood. I had to hang window coverings, paint, put in gardens, and figure out how to fix things on my own. I was learning how to balance home ownership with working a full-time job. Several months after moving in, two friends of mine introduced me to Richard. We hit it off, and he eventually moved into the house with me.

Harleigh Ann and Sugar, now in their middle years, didn't have much interest in exploring the great outdoors any longer. Miss Piggy, several years older and in failing health, rarely went out. She began to show her age and became bone thin, plus she had a kidney disease and thyroid issues. I soon had to let her go, as she became more and more miserable. Her previous owner would have been pleased with the long life she lived.

At my new house, I would sometimes leave my front door open while running in and out. One day, after running groceries in, I noticed an orange tabby in my kitchen. He was a kitten and friendly. I let him stay for a while, and he left whenever he felt like it. I became accustomed to my new friend and enjoyed his brief stays. He disappeared for a few weeks, and when he reappeared, he cautiously approached me in my front yard. I noticed something had sliced the tip off one of his ears. I later learned of a group that catches feral cats, neuters them, and then clips their ear as documentation. The cats are then released into the neighborhood from which they came.

We went in the house, and he decided he wasn't going to leave. Richard named him Dude. Dude had a friendly disposition and had no problem getting along with Harleigh Ann or any human beings. But Sugar was a challenge for him. She didn't like Dude; she tolerated him. I still wanted a dog, but I would need to find one that could get along with my cats.

On a late September afternoon, I went to a shelter in search of my first dog. Cool temperatures, falling leaves, and sunshine made it a pleasant day. I was hopeful and anxious to find a dog to call my own. This particular shelter was just that—a shelter and not much more. It was an old building set near an interstate overpass and a log yard. The area was in a state of urban decay, and there was a homeless shelter nearby. I guess it's fitting to have homeless dogs housed next to homeless people. The desperation must be the same.

Inside were rows of stalls created with cinderblocks and cyclone-fence gates. The runs were concrete with drains in the center. Informational sheets on the available dogs hung on the stalls. If a stall didn't have an informational sheet, it was because the dog was on stray hold or on hold for a rescue pickup.

Walking down the rows, I saw so many choices: desperate dogs, sad dogs, happy-to-see-you dogs, and dogs pacing in their cells. One dog caught my eye, but not because he was adorable or trying to get me to take him home. He was the opposite: a stoic ten-year-old dog lying on an elevated bed, staring at the cinderblock wall. It looked to me like he had given up on life. He was large with the black-and-tan markings and physical traits of a German shepherd. He seemed to have another bloodline, giving him a softer, more rounded snout.

When I stopped at his stall, he glanced in my direction with his sad amber eyes then turned and looked away again. I didn't impress him. A volunteer approached me and asked me if I wanted to take him out, since it was about time for his walk. She too didn't display much enthusiasm.

I wondered how long he had been at the shelter and how many people had passed him by. Despite his lack of enthusiasm and my quickly degrading mood, I took him out of his concrete run and outside. He didn't appear to care much for me at all. He took care of business, stared into the open space beyond the fence, and turned to go back to his cell. The information sheet said his name was Snickers. It also said he was at the shelter, not as a stray but as an owner surrender. Perhaps his mood was due to his owner leaving him at the shelter at ten years of age. There was no information on his sheet about whether or not he got along with cats.

Snickers was on sale the day I went searching, a Sunday during football season. Like me or not, he was going home with me. I couldn't bear the thought of this old man sleeping one more night in a shelter. I knew no one else would want him with his apathetic attitude, so he became mine.

We walked out of the shelter. He stared straight ahead and seemed to be excited to go for a walk outdoors. When I opened my car door, a two-door sedan, he jumped right into the backseat and didn't give the shelter another look. He was out of there, and he knew it. I decided I would keep the name *Snickers*. I didn't feel he needed to learn a new name at that point in his life.

He loved to ride in cars, but he wasn't going to let me know it yet. On the drive home, he sat in the back seat, looking straight ahead out the window. I would look in the rear-view mirror and wonder if he would ever like me. And would he like my cats?

Snickers came in the house and immediately headed for a corner, where he lay down. Was this how he lived in his old house? Was this his way of telling me, "Thanks, but I'm still not sure about you"? I petted him to try to reassure him. He ignored my touch, and it wasn't easing his anxiety. I noticed a large lump the size of a softball underneath his left foreleg. I wondered if this was why he was so cheap. Regardless, I wasn't taking him back. I called my vet and made an appointment to have Snickers checked out.

He was a polite dog. He didn't jump up, he didn't bark, he didn't cause any problems at all. He was more apathetic about the cats then he was about me. One time—and only one time—Snickers lost his temper with one of my cats. I fed him in the kitchen, and Dude decided he would check out the food in Snickers's bowl while Snickers was eating. Snickers took offense and bit Dude in the head. Most cats have a healthy fear of dogs. Dude didn't. He had been a stray but wasn't a dog-savvy cat. As a matter of fact, Dude didn't fear much of anything. He took his lumps and carried on like nothing had happened. But he never again tested

Snickers's willingness to share his food.

I decided Snickers needed to know this was his new house and there were new rules. I grabbed his collar and led him to the couch. Up on the couch he went, and he finally relaxed. He would lie on the couch with his head hanging over the edge. I would sit below him and pet him. As we shared this time, I thought he might be considering giving me a chance. He liked the couch, and he stayed there most days.

I put Snickers in a spare room when I went to work, and he let me know how much he hated it. He would whine, breaking my heart as I tried to get out the door. I took care of his comforts, but maybe he thought each time I left would be the last time he saw me. The heartbreak he must have felt as a senior dog abandoned at a shelter was palpable.

The time came for Snickers's checkup. My cats had all been to this vet, and now Snickers was about to meet the staff. The office was a small, rustic building, and the reception area was a little too dark. The common area, where dogs and cats shared space, was neat and complete with outdated magazines. The staff was familiar with me, but not with Snickers. The receptionist gave him a genuine smile when she greeted him. I was secretly pleased he gave her the same cold shoulder he had given me when we met. After Snickers's exam, the vet said that the lump was most likely a fatty deposit common in shepherds and that I shouldn't worry about it. So I didn't.

Snickers and I would go on long walks in the neighborhood. He loved his walks more than he loved riding in a car. No sooner did I put on my sneakers than he would coo in anticipation, extending his neck in an almost howl. Snickers was protective of me on our walks. He would warn strangers off if he felt they were a threat to me. I wasn't sure what his criteria was for judging a threat, but I was happy he felt a need to protect me.

If I ever went anywhere without Snickers, he would complain. He didn't suffer from separation anxiety in the sense that he would get destructive. Rather, he seemed to fear that I wouldn't return. Our bond was growing and our love deepening.

One month after Snickers came to live with us, Richard and I went out of town for Thanksgiving. I didn't want to leave Snickers alone, and boarding him at a kennel was out of the question. The last thing I wanted was for Snickers to feel abandoned again. I found a pet sitter to stay with him. When we met, I liked her right away. She was pretty, with a kind face, genuine smile, and long, flowing brown hair. She was knowledgeable and kind. Cleaning cat boxes and walking Snickers were no problem for her. She also promised to spend extra time with him, playing ball.

Richard and I came home a little early from the trip and found the sitter sitting on the floor. Snickers was by her side, and she was writing out notes for me. When he saw me, he was so happy he almost forgot his manners and started to jump up on me. I was thrilled. Snickers liked me—even loved me! His joy was overwhelming, but I still managed to capture the moment by taking a picture with my cell phone. It is my most cherished photo of him.

The day soon came when Snickers love for walks wasn't stronger than whatever was going on in his body. Shortly into one of our walks, his head dropped, and his breathing became labored. I knew something was wrong, and I suspected it had to do with the lump in his side. I made another appointment for him.

When the day came, Snickers took his now standard position in the car: his back legs on the back seat and his front legs on my armrest. He was attentive and always eager to go for a ride.

The petite, dark-haired receptionist greeted us in her typical kind and compassionate manner. Snickers was patient but more interested in the sights and especially of the sounds of dogs barking in the background. A different vet worked with Snickers this time. I liked him better than the female vet, as he seemed to take a more serious approach to Snickers's issues. He was also warm and kind. I demanded he do more than make assumptions, and he told me he would take a biopsy and run some tests.

This meant I had to leave Snickers at the office, which I hated doing. I'm sure it was traumatic for him to see me turn my back on him and walking away. When I returned to pick him up, the vet told me they had done a biopsy of the lump. Snickers had a bandage wrapped around his chest to cover the hole they'd made in his side. We drove back home and waited for the diagnosis, which would take a couple of days. I was ready to do whatever it took to fix this for Snickers.

Life moved along, and Richard became my fiancée. We hated living in a house where we could reach out the window and touch the neighbor's house. So we decided to search for vacant land. The search was extensive, since there wasn't much vacant, buildable land left in the area. The plots that hadn't sold were usually vacant because the land didn't drain, the water was bad, or some other issue.

We stumbled upon five acres near Richard's hometown. There had been a house on the land, which homesteaders had built in the early 1920s. The land hadn't been well cared for, shown by the empty liquor bottles spread about the property. The vegetation was overgrown, and primitive fences were down in various parts of the property.

I took Snickers for a ride out to see our future home. Richard had already headed out to the property. On the way to there, I received a phone call from the vet. I can still hear his voice telling me, "We don't have all the results back, but the preliminary tests show a lot of bone matter in the sample. That usually means bone cancer."

I was stunned. A lump suddenly showed up in my throat. It felt like pieces of my broken heart. I couldn't breathe, much less talk. Snickers kept vigilant watch out the window, unaware of the death sentence.

The vet could tell I was upset, because I didn't respond. I couldn't without losing my composure. He was kind enough not to expect me to say much. He told me bone cancer is a fast-moving cancer, and Snickers didn't have long. We ended the conversation, which had broken my heart.

I continued to the new property, trying to maintain my composure when all I wanted to do was cry. Snickers ran around and explored his new surroundings. The foundation of the house wasn't dug, but the footprint was laid out. The rest of the property was a mess of overgrown trees and vegetation. Snickers was content and happy, sniffing the people and critters that had been there. Of course, he was oblivious to his dire diagnosis. Anyway, unlike humans, dogs don't get depressed thinking of what they're going to miss. They live in the moment and live each moment to its fullest, appreciating the gift that is life.

On our way back home, I stopped and bought us greasy burgers and french fries. When we arrived home, I sat on the tile kitchen floor with Snickers, and we had lunch. I figured if his time was short, he was going to have whatever his heart desired, and it desired a burger and fries.

Ever the polite dog, Snickers sat in front of me but didn't dig into the bag. He sat, staring at my hands, drool threatening to drop. I unwrapped his burger and set it on the opened wrapper on the floor. It didn't take him long to finish his burger. I was taking a bit longer, so I hand-fed him fries so I could catch up. Snickers's eyes never left my hands, which continuously produced fries.

I now knew why his former owners had dumped him at the shelter: because he was sick. He was old and full of cancer. Could they not bring themselves to put him down or watch him die? Or did he turn out to be too expensive for them? Regardless, I vowed to fill the rest of his days with all the love I could possibly give him.

The doctor was right: bone cancer, or osteosarcoma, moves very fast. The hole they made in Snickers, which was dime-sized and right under his shoulder, wouldn't heal or stop bleeding. One night, a few days after the biopsy, I woke up to find Snickers sitting next to my bed. He was dripping blood through his bandage, and panting. His head was erect, but his eyelids were heavy. What could I do to comfort him?

I took him back to his bed in the kitchen, where I had placed it, since blood is easier to clean off tile than carpet. I sat with him, trying to find a place to pet him where it wouldn't hurt. Finally, his panting slowed a bit. Although he was miserable and lethargic due to chronic pain, Snickers never lashed out or tried to bite me while I comforted him.

The next day, I took Snickers to the vet to get his bandage changed. My heart was heavy with concern for him. He maintained his copilot position with his back feet on the back seat, front feet on the armrest, and gaze fixed out the window.

When the technician took Snickers's leash from me, Snickers and I took a long look at each other. He didn't want to go with the tech, and I didn't want to leave him. As we looked at each other, he stepped toward me. Many unspoken words passed between us in that long look. The tech encouraged him to come with her. I told her to make sure he got to go outside and relieve himself. She smiled and said she would, then told Snickers to come on. He turned and went with her.

I had to go to work, so the arrangement was to have Richard pick Snickers up after he left work. I called Richard and told him Snickers probably wouldn't stop bleeding. He said it was likely getting to be time to put him to sleep, and I agreed. What I didn't know was that a tragic miscommunication had just occurred.

Later in the evening, I found a moment when I could take a break. I called Richard, wanting to check on Snickers. I was hopeful he was having a better evening. Richard said, "I thought you understood it was time for him to be put down." I was shocked. Instead of being picked up at night, Snickers was put to sleep. Alone again, abandoned again. But this time, I had done it to him. I wasn't ready to let him go. I hadn't even said good-bye. I asked if he at least went in the room with Snickers. He said no.

I had let Snickers down after he had learned to trust me. I couldn't bear to stay at work. And my line of work required my full attention; any distraction could be deadly. I called my boss, who was a dog lover too. I told him what happened, and he told me to go home.

The drive home was a blur. I was on autopilot, fighting

back the tears. My heart was broken to a degree I had never experienced. I had let my dog down—with deadly consequences. I parked my car and shut it down, all from muscle memory. That night, there would be no Snickers lifting his head off the couch, making me feel welcome in a way only a dog can. I went in the house and didn't say much to Richard. I changed and then just sat on my couch, staring at the wall, tears flowing freely, listening to the quiet left by Snickers. I had no idea I could love so hard, so fast. Most of all, I was very upset to have let my new best friend down with tragic, irreversible consequences.

A couple of days later, I was eating lunch with my friend Cole, a coworker and a fellow dog lover. Neither of us had brought lunch to work, so we found a place to grab a quick bite. We have a special connection, as if we have been friends all our lives. Cole has a serious disposition, but his kindness shows through his warm smile and gentle manners. I always feel a sense of peace when I'm around him. He is kind, compassionate, and honest with himself and always striving to be a better person. Not once has he failed to be kind and supportive of me. We share many of the same philosophies on life, religion, and work. I can trust him with my feelings, which I share with a rare few.

I detailed the past day's events, and he told me he had recently lost a dog that also had bone cancer and went quickly. He shared his heartbreak when he had to carry his dog to the vet because he could no longer walk. When I told him I was guilt-ridden about letting Snickers down, he said to me with all sincerity, "Don't you know all dogs go to heaven?" Once again, my friend had the perfect words to say to me so my heart could begin to heal. We chatted for a bit, finished our meals, then went back to work at our fast-paced jobs.

It gave me great comfort to envision Snickers exploring heaven pain-free. I was sure he forgave me, because dogs know only the purest form of love: nonjudgmental and forgiving. Now I needed to forgive myself, and that would take time—lots of time. I still haven't completely forgiven myself.

In the meantime, run free, sweet boy. When I come to see you, please jump on me all you want. I love you, Snickers.

CHAPTER 2

Panzer the Neurotic One

I missed Snickers, and I often cried when I thought of him. I tried to move forward, but I missed the unconditional love he gave. I thought of him often, and I didn't know when it would be appropriate to get another dog. Although Snickers's story ended tragically almost as soon as it began, I was determined to find happiness with another dog.

I started reading a book about dogs, their emotions, and their ability to love. The word for assigning human emotions to animal behavior is *anthropomorphism*. Scientists must find animal lovers to be a silly lot. I don't believe dogs think like humans or process information the same way humans do. But I also don't believe dogs function solely on an instinctual level. I believe they have emotions. I also believe dogs have the capacity to love. They are far better at love than most humans. Dogs don't judge us. They forgive us when we wrong them, and they stand by our side regardless of our many flaws.

I finished the book and decided to get another dog. I couldn't recall a time when I'd ever felt unconditionally loved other than with Snickers. I needed to have that love in my life again.

I had heard that if a dog is raised with cats, chances are it will get along with all cats. I also heard a submissive dog won't rush up to you and demand attention. Armed with this information, off to the shelter I went, in search of a puppy. It was a crisp, colorful fall day in the Pacific Northwest.

I wasn't yet aware of the many online websites available for researching available animals. So I wasn't sure of what I would find. I hated going to the shelter. They couldn't have chosen a more dreadful, desolate part of the city to house throwaway dogs. (The shelter eventually moved to a beautiful place close to a river.)

As I approached the shelter, my thoughts turned to Snickers and our freedom ride. I resolved that if there was another Snickers there—an old, sick, abandoned dog—I would take it home instead of looking for a puppy.

Just as I walked in the door to where the dogs were kept, I spotted him. He was in the first stall, a strategic move on the part of the shelter. He was a three-month-old puppy, thirty pounds, black and tan, and the only puppy in the shelter. Puppies have an extremely easy time finding their way out of shelters. Everyone wants a puppy, it seems. This puppy's information page said animal control had found him wandering near the interstate in a densely populated area.

When I arrived, he was lying on his back with his paws pulled up to his shoulders. He looked calm, peaceful, and content, and he didn't bother to get up to greet me. The information tag said he was part shepherd and part Rottweiler. This was going to be a large dog. If no one stepped forward to claim him within the three-day holding period, he would be available for adoption.

When the pup's three days were up, I made sure I was at the shelter when they opened. I was ready to bring a dog home. As it turned out, I had competition. There was one other person at the shelter who wanted him. Not being sure what would happen, I prepared to look for another dog. I wasn't emotionally attached to the puppy, but I was going to be disappointed if I wasn't able to walk away with him that day. I didn't want to go without a dog any longer.

Just as the other adopter was about to get the puppy, one of the shelter workers asked me which dog I was there for, and I told her the puppy. The way the shelter handled multiple people choosing the same dog was to do a raffle. We stood there and waited while the staff pulled a ticket. I wasn't expecting to win, but I did.

The cute puppy was now mine, but he had to be neutered before he could go home with me. The shelter scheduled the surgery the following week at a local animal hospital, and I was allowed to be there on the day of his surgery. He was a hit with the staff. His favorite pose—rolling on his back and pulling his front paws to his chest—became his information folder photo.

I was asked to pick a name for him. To honor what I believed to be his German heritage and his potential size, I named him Panzer—a tank used by Germans during World War II. Richard had to pick up Panzer when he was ready, because I was at work. He later called me, complaining that Panzer had thrown up not once but twice in his truck on the ride home. I laughed, but not out loud. It wasn't immediately clear if Panzer was carsick or if he was just recovering from his surgery.

Panzer soon grew into his name. He was a large, sturdy dog and didn't seem to mind my cats. The cats weren't impressed but were curious about Panzer; as a puppy, he was closer to their size than Snickers ever was. Panzer didn't love them, but he wouldn't be killing them either.

When he was five months old, it was time to move into the house in the country. As it turned out, Panzer had horrible carsickness. Nothing I tried alleviated it for him. I tried fresh air on his face, letting him ride in the front, letting him ride in the back, and even an herbal remedy. Some dogs grow out of it, but some do not.

During the trip to his new home, we tried to keep Panzer's discomfort to a minimum. We tied him to the back of the truck bed so he couldn't jump out and couldn't wander in the back of the truck. He fared pretty well, not throwing up on the thirty-mile drive—until the truck stopped.

Before we could get Panzer out, I saw the look on his face change. His body was still, his forehead was crinkled, and the corners of his mouth were pulled back. He then emptied the contents of his stomach. I felt so bad for him. I despise vomiting, and I'm sure it isn't a pleasant experience for a dog either.

At our country home, Panzer loved the open spaces, the endless opportunities to explore, and the family to call his own. He was a smart dog and responded quickly to potty training, with minimal accidents in the house.

One of Panzer's issues, which came to light at our new home, was his dislike of young children. He wasn't a fan of running or screaming or any combination of the two. I didn't have children, so this information came the hard way. There were a few young children in the area that would walk by on their way home. Panzer would run down the fence line, barking furiously at them.

Richard became my husband in the summer of 2006. Panzer was oblivious of the wedding preparations and seemed to enjoy the visiting adult family members. The ceremony was at the house, and Panzer stayed in the garage for most of the festivities. I gave him frequent breaks, and he was happy to be away from all the people and the noise. He was nearing one year of age and was still developing in size and personality.

During the most important part of his upbringing, I got assigned to work the graveyard. It's a horrible shift for me. I worked the shift for many years but never was able to make a comfortable adjustment to it. I commend those who thrive on it. My body and eyes especially want to be sleeping at night. I hadn't asked for the graveyard shift, and I wouldn't have brought a puppy into my life if I'd known I was going to be working nights. Graveyard shift is hard on any dog, especially one full of energy and in the developmental stage of its life.

When I was home during the day, I was asleep. When I worked, Richard was home, and he was asleep. Panzer wasn't getting the attention, training, or stimulation he needed. Many days I woke up to a chewed-up mess. Candles, shoes, and anything else not picked up is fair game to any puppy. I felt terrible for Panzer. I didn't mind the messes, but I didn't want to wake up to a sick or injured dog. A solution to the problem escaped me. I needed to sleep, and Panzer needed to be taken care of. The thought of adding another dog to keep Panzer company while I slept seemed to be a good idea.

CHAPTER 3

Ruby the Princess

A coworker mentioned to me he had a friend who was looking to get rid of a dog. I asked him what the problem was with the dog, because the last thing I needed was a problematic dog. He didn't know the answer to that question, so he worked on getting the owner and I together.

My coworker had his friend come in one night to talk to me about the dog. He told me he and his girlfriend didn't have time to care for her as she should be cared for. They were both gone long hours, and the dog wasn't getting the attention she deserved. I told him to bring the dog over, and I would let the two of them meet and see if they liked each other.

Then the day came—one special day in the springtime. Flowers were blooming, and the skies were typically cloudy. When Ruby arrived, it had temporarily stopped raining, and the love of Panzer's life appeared before him. She was a beautiful Springer spaniel mix with long, flowing white and black hair. When I say long hair, I mean *really* long hair. The hair on her tail was so long it nearly touched the ground. She was a medium-sized dog, approximately seventy pounds, with a soft face, dark-brown eyes, and floppy ears.

She got out of her car and pranced right up to Panzer. He instantly fell head over heels. They ran and chased each other, and Panzer forgot I existed. Now I could sleep during the day.

Ruby's owner was a tall, slim redhead with short hair and ivory skin accented with a little makeup and bright-green eyes. She was mild mannered but protective of Ruby. She wasn't ready to leave her with me until she was certain I would love her as much as she did. She hugged Ruby and cried hard when she left. My heart broke for her. I couldn't imagine giving up a dog I loved as much as she clearly loved Ruby. Panzer, on the other hand, was very pleased.

Ruby came to us well mannered and trained in basic commands. She even liked cats. Well, truthfully, she liked to tease cats and try to get them to play with her. She also would chase them or stick her nose on them. None of this was well received by the cats. It was as if I could see her joy when a cat ran from her aggravations only to be chased by her.

Panzer didn't take part in the teasing. Instead, he attempted to turn Ruby's attention to him. All he wanted was for her to play with him, run with him, chase him, and dote on him. Ruby was usually gentle and always a princess. Everyone who saw her remarked on her beauty. She knew it too. She would sit in front of visitors and look lovingly into their eyes. Their sole purpose was to pet her and dote on her. If they forgot she was there, she would gently put a paw on their leg to remind them. Maybe Princess or Diva would have been a better name for her.

Panzer was happy, and the challenges were fewer, so I was happy also. Ruby and Panzer played, roughhoused, fought once in a while, but mostly became the best of friends. They were never far from each other's side. Ruby would often chase Panzer and run into him, bowling him over. Panzer's response was to expose his belly, inciting her to play more. The pair of them would explore, chasing birds, digging holes, and sniffing the scent of some critter that had walked the yard at night. If ever there were two dogs made for each other, it was those two.

Ruby's lone issue was extreme possessiveness of her food. I don't know why she had this trait, since she was never deprived of food. Sometimes this is indicative of resource guarding, but she wasn't possessive of any other belonging. The few fights she picked were always about food. If she was being fed or a scrap fell on the floor, it was hers. If she had a treat, she would growl if Panzer got too close. If he decided to try anyhow, he learned a lesson the hard way.

Ruby also made it clear she was the only female dog allowed in a rather large radius around her castle. Many country dwellers don't contain their dogs on their property. One dog that wandered the neighborhood was a female husky. She had the full, heavy coat of a husky in the red version. And she had the same hierarchy beliefs Ruby held. She was the queen of the neighborhood.

One day, the husky got past our primitive fencing and wandered onto our property—all the way up to the house. Ruby, Panzer, and I didn't know she was there when we walked out of the house. Ruby spotted her and lost her mind along with her temper. She crouched, barked, and then pounced on the husky. A few bites were all it took to convince the husky she'd made a mistake. She turned and ran, but Ruby was in full meltdown.

I told Panzer to stay, which he did, and I attempted to regain control of my angry princess. I tried to chase after her, but my speed will never compare to that of an angry dog. The husky ran through the fence with Ruby hot on her heels. Ruby was going too fast and overshot the road. She fell into a drop-off, tumbled like an Olympic gymnast, landed on her feet, and bounced right out of the drop-off. The husky gained the time and distance it needed to make it home to safety. Between my chuckles, I was as able to yell to Ruby to stop. She did and barked, no doubt telling the husky, "And don't come back!" She pranced back to me.

About six months later, I went to work, and Ruby's mom's boyfriend was there. He told me his girlfriend was regretting her choice and would take Ruby back if we didn't want her. I told him that we did want her and that Panzer was deeply attached to her. He told me he would pass along the message.

I panicked. I didn't know if this woman was going to come back and take Ruby or demand I give her back. She was her original owner, after all, and we didn't have anything that would make her mine legally. All I had was a lovesick dog.

I decided I would get another dog in case Ruby's past owner demanded her back. I knew that owner loved her, and I wouldn't be able to tell her no if she told me she needed her dog back. I never heard from her, and I hope that she trusted Ruby was in good hands and was loved.

CHAPTER 4

Cowboy the Pack Clown

My work partner, the same one who brought Ruby into my life, told me about some mastiff pups up for adoption in the county just to the north of mine. He didn't have any other information. It was getting close to Richard's birthday, and I asked him if he would like a mastiff puppy for his birthday. Richard had wanted a mastiff, because he liked the breed, but he wasn't going to buy one from a breeder. He restrained his enthusiasm but was looking forward to going to the shelter.

It is a low-kill shelter in a rural area that's mostly farmlands. They don't fund animal control, so animals show up at their door in many ways. On a rainy fall day, we drove half an hour to get there. It's not far off the interstate in an isolated, quiet area full of trees—in stark contrast to the other shelter.

We pulled up to the shelter and got out of the car. We heard dogs barking in the distance. The reception area was full of cat cages, some with multiple cats. Dogs were in runs to the left of the room. I couldn't see into the runs, but I could hear some dogs barking. We asked the receptionist where we could find the mastiff puppies. A volunteer took us to a room past the cats, where the puppies were in an enclosed circular pen.

Puppy training pads and newspaper lined the pen. Six black

pups surrounded us as we sat on the floor of the shelter. Adorable pups with oversized heads and paws and clumsy gaits all vied for our attention. We were shown a picture of their mother, who was in foster care. She was a beautiful copper-brown dog with a huge head. Somehow she'd managed to produce all black puppies. This was going to be Richard's birthday present, so I let him decide which one he wanted. He decided on a male that kept pestering him for attention, and he named him Cowboy.

Cowboy came home after being neutered. I expected Ruby to have some maternal instincts toward this mild-mannered puppy. I was wrong. She was beyond apathetic. She wasn't happy to have to split the attention she believed should be all hers. She wouldn't let him near her and would walk away if Cowboy tried to interact with her. He wasn't offended and kept trying to impress her.

However, Panzer made it *clear* he didn't like this new guy. He would growl and snap if Cowboy got near him. He never played with Cowboy or allowed him to come near him.

Cowboy was a funny-looking puppy with a huge head and paws. A large bone protruded from the front of his head, giving him a Frankensteinish look. I asked the vet about the bone. These were his eyebrows, he informed me, and he would grow into them in a year or so.

Cowboy did grow into those eyebrows and those paws. He became a handsome, bigheaded, barrel-chested dog with a big heart to match. His sweet temperament endeared him to all who met him. Cowboy was the master of the head tilt, which no dog owner is immune to. He used it often and made me laugh at his goofy personality. When he perked up those ears and crinkled his forehead and tilted his head from side to side, I was putty in his hands.

Parts of my property would hold water in the fall and spring. There Cowboy spent hours on end standing in one of these large puddles, staring at the water, watching the bugs jump. This bug-hunting technique served Cowboy well when hunting for moles.

He would sniff mole holes until he found one with a fresh scent. He would then hover over it for however long it took him to see movement. Then he would pounce and come out with his prize. Cowboy was long on patience, which won him many field mice and moles.

Although full of heart, Cowboy was short on courage. Everything new was scary to him. The first time he saw fog, he sat there barking as if he'd lost his way. If new people came to the house, Cowboy would bark a deep, ferocious bark. He would then run to the farthest corner of the yard and continue to bark at the trespassers. It was as if he were pleading to the strangers not to come any closer, because he had nowhere else to run. Once the trespassers were in the house, Cowboy found courage to meet his new friend.

Despite hours of amusement provided by Cowboy, Panzer was not impressed. He didn't like Cowboy, and he made sure he knew. Most of the time, Panzer would ignore him. But at times he attacked him for reasons unknown to me. Cowboy wouldn't fight back. I wasn't dog savvy enough at the time to know what drove Panzer's behaviors. I talked to lots of dog savvy people I knew, but none of them could offer any suggestions for handling Panzer.

Richard would get mad at Panzer and in his frustration tell me he was a dangerous dog and needed to be put down. But I refused to give up on Panzer. I would find the right person to help me with him. I had to. I owed it to him. I had brought him to my house and given him a home and a pack. I was going to exhaust all means before I considered any other option.

Through it all, Cowboy remained a sweet and loving dog. His most endearing trait was that he remained a puppy at heart. He ran with stiff legs when chasing a ball, he arched his neck when he pawed at me, and he was always good-natured. He would lie on a chair or the couch and look up at me with those vast brown eyes as content as he could be.

One summer evening, I had a visit from a friend who brought along her female pug. She and I sat on the back deck and let her old, almost blind pug and Cowboy play. The pug strutted her feminine wiles for her new audience, and my friend laughed so hard. She had never seen her act that way. Cowboy bought every bit of what the little girl was selling. He followed her around and cooed, trying to impress this little gal a tenth his size. He couldn't get enough of her. He was great with other dogs, male or female. He would play with the males and fall in love with the females.

I'm an avid gardener, both landscape and vegetables. Cowboy, on the other hand, is an avid vegetable hunter. My nemesis in the vegetable garden was the green pepper. I had no luck getting those pepper plants to bear fruit. One year, I had a beauty of a pepper growing, and I was looking forward to eating that pepper. It needed about another week before it would be perfect. One day I was gardening, and my pride dictated taking another look at the pepper. When I looked, it was gone. My one and only pepper. *Crunch, crunch* was what I heard. Cowboy had noticed the pepper too. For him, it was just right; it didn't need another week. From then on, a fence would surround my vegetable garden.

People remained an issue for Cowboy. I saw him completely unafraid of only two people who came to the house. They were both large, one a man and one a woman. The male was dark skinned, short, with short dark hair. The female was light skinned, tall, with long light-brown hair. The only thing they had in common was their easygoing personalities and size. Cowboy kept me guessing who he would be comfortable seeing for the first time.

There was one person he didn't bark at: a neighbor I trust completely, Angela. She lived close by with her husband and menagerie of animals. She was my emergency handler when I couldn't get home and the dogs needed potty breaks. I gave her the run of the house, and I never had cause to doubt my decision.

She would almost always bring treats with her when she came to visit. It took her coming over only a few times, loaded with treats, for Cowboy to look forward to her visits. He would run up to her, tail wagging, bounding from side to side, to greet her. She didn't incite barking and running to the farthest corner of the yard.

CHAPTER 5

Lenny the Gentle Soul

For reasons even I don't understand, I continued to glance at listings of dogs looking for homes. Shelters and rescues were now posting available dogs online. For someone like me, that was a recipe for trouble. I have a love for large dogs and especially rescue dogs. I want to save them all. One day I happened upon an ad for a Bluetick hound crossed with a Great Dane, which a rescue group had listed.

I made an appointment to meet the dog. I had e-mailed the rescues leader, and she agreed to bring the dog so I could meet him. We were to meet outside a pet supply store in the county where I rescued Cowboy.

It was nighttime, and the parking lot was almost empty. I saw a tall, middle-aged man with brown hair walking toward the store with a long-legged dog. I decided this must be the person I was going to meet. The dog was a gigantic black-and-white one with a spotted chest and paws. The picture I'd seen of the dog made it look like it had blue hair. I then realized the picture was overexposed. The dog hung its head and walked right into the glass door before the man from the rescue could open it. The man later explained he thought the dog might have some sight issues.

Once inside the store, he offered to let me walk around with

Lenny. Being a large dog, he didn't do well on the tile floor. He slipped and slid while keeping his head down as we walked. He didn't care to know who had ahold of the other end of his leash. Not once did he look up at me or show interest in me. I was familiar with this approach.

The rescuer told me he thought the dog might also be somewhat deaf, because he didn't appear to listen and didn't respond to commands. Oh, and by the way, he said Lenny experienced seizures, which were controlled by medication. He also loved food and would get into any food—dog food or otherwise—if left unattended.

The rescuer told me if I wanted him, I could have him, and he wouldn't charge the usual fee. He said the dog had so many problems—blind, deaf, seizures, and urinary issues—and was old at seven years of age. For a giant breed dog, seven years is pretty close to the end of the life span. It says a lot about our society that we see the elderly and the impaired as broken and not as worthy as the rest of us. The belief is magnified if the subject of our judgments is an animal. I paid full price for the dog he called Lenny.

The rescuer told me Lenny had been found as a stray and was emaciated and full of scars from being bitten by other dogs. I could only imagine how frightening it must have been for him, a shy dog, lost, having seizures, not finding food, and attacked by other dogs. When Lenny was caught, his new home became the shelter. No one came for him.

I don't know what shelter he was in, but they were getting ready to have him euthanized for space. His savior, a kind-hearted woman who was partial to large dogs, picked him up just before his scheduled euthanasia. Lenny's savior took him home to live with her dog, but her dog was terminally ill, and Lenny made him anxious. So Lenny moved again, this time into the rescue. At least he was safe. I would find out later how misunderstood he was.

By paying full price for Lenny, I felt I was buying back some of his dignity. His parting words to me were that Lenny wouldn't do his business while on a leash, and he was probably pretty ready for a break. Lenny hung his head as we walked out of the store, and I had plans to make sure he never hung his head in despair again.

When we got home, I let Lenny out for a break, but he just wandered around, nose to the ground. After a few minutes, I brought him back into the house. I didn't want him to wander too much, since the driveway didn't have a gate.

There was a lot to learn about Lenny's peculiarities. After watching him for a while, I discovered he covered great distances before finding the exact right spot to relieve himself. The first night in the house wasn't a good one for Lenny. He was uncomfortable with being in a new place—particular about where he would lie down. His first evening, he paced and whined, but by the next day, he understood he was home. He didn't make giant strides. He made baby steps with lots of reassurance.

Lenny was a quiet, solemn dog. He didn't bark, and he always appeared sleepy. I made an appointment with the vet to have him checked out and his medication needs evaluated. When the day came, and it was time to load Lenny into my truck, I pulled up the folding seat so he could stand or sit behind the front seats. He didn't sit. He stood and stared out the side window the entire ride.

When we got into town, I parked in the veterinarian's small parking lot. Lenny fumbled out of my truck. He didn't seem to have a good grasp of how to walk gracefully on those long legs. We walked toward the office door, with Lenny's head hanging, and he walked right into the glass door. I opened the door for him, feeling like a failure. The receptionist, a large, gray-haired woman, had jumped out of her seat, which was facing the door. Since the office had a small reception area, she had a full view of my ineptness. She was sympathetic to Lenny and offered him a treat, which he didn't want. He hadn't hit his head too hard and didn't seem affected.

Getting Lenny on the scale was easy. He was gentle and

would do whatever he was directed to do. Looking back, I remembered he didn't even give his rescuer a second glance when we walked out the door. It could be Lenny had taken off from his house on his own. But this fact remained: no one came looking for him. I will never know how he came to be a stray.

We were put into the dog waiting room, which was just off the reception area. As we waited there, Lenny relaxed, sniffing around the small office. The vet, a middle-aged, tall, thin, white-haired man with a gentle disposition, came in, and Lenny greeted him with his usual apathy. The vet was kind and gentle with Lenny, as he has always been with all my animals. With Lenny's easygoing temperament, a person could do about anything to him, and he would put up with it.

This made it easy for the vet to check him out but harder to assess whether he had any hearing or sight issues. The vet adjusted Lenny's medication, taking him off phenobarbital and adjusting the dosage of the potassium bromide. This would make Lenny less lethargic and yet keep the seizures at bay. As for the other issues, the vet said there didn't appear to be any.

Cowboy and Ruby didn't care for Lenny. They didn't interact with him in a positive or a negative way; they just ignored him. Cowboy liked a more energetic, youthful dog to play with. Panzer would sometimes attack Lenny, just as he did Cowboy. Lenny wouldn't fight back, just as Cowboy wouldn't. Lenny would hit the ground, roll onto his back, let out a pathetic whine, and pee on himself. It was heartbreaking to see.

I would always end those attacks immediately and discipline Panzer, but it didn't seem to affect Panzer's behavior at all. Richard would fly into a rage if Panzer attacked Lenny, reminding me that he wanted Panzer put down. I still refused to give up on him.

I learned fast that there wasn't a thing wrong with Lenny's sight or hearing. His head-hanging was due to lack of confidence. In time he no longer walked with a hung head unless he had his nose to the ground on one of his exploratory walks. He also no longer walked into doors. He held his head up and waited for me to open the door before rushing across the threshold.

I figured out he could hear just fine by opening the cookie jar while he was in the living room. I saw his head snap to attention in my direction. He wasn't fooling me. Lenny was just going to do what he wanted to do. After a while, even if he were an acre away, he would perk up his ears, lift his head, and come running at a full gallop toward the sound of his name.

Lenny was particular about his chosen sleeping locations. The couch in the living room was such a favorite, he broke down the seat in his favorite spot. He also liked a particular bed. If another dog was in his spot on the couch or the bed, he would either just jump onto his spot or whine until I moved the offender.

Lenny stepped on Cowboy more than once. Cowboy's reaction was hilarious, most likely only to me. He would awake dazed, eyes wide, ears pulled back, looking at me as if he needed me to explain what had happened.

The one female dog of the pack, Ruby, peaked Lenny's interest. It took some time, but once he was sure Ruby wouldn't attack him, he began checking her out. He started following her around often, sniffing her behind. She wouldn't give him attention, but she didn't chase him away either.

Lenny was also an avid chewer. He liked to chew on rubber balls, but often he preferred Richard's shoes or mine. He didn't do much damage, so we would let him chew on the rubber soles until he started to wear away at them. Lenny was a calm, peaceful, angelic presence in our lives.

CHAPTER 6

The Times and the Tides

The house I had built was in a flood zone. I researched the area before purchasing the land by using a Federal Emergency Management Agency (FEMA) map. The map labeled the area zone X, meaning it was known to flood once every one hundred years. I believed I would be safe, since the area had flooded well within the past one hundred years. I soon learned neither FEMA nor the county updated their maps frequently.

The property flooded the first year we were in the house. November through January are stressful months when living in our floodplain. These are the peak months for the property to flood, and "How much?" is always the question. During my first flood experience, the house was surrounded by water. It reached to the garage pad and stayed approximately ten feet from the perimeter of the house. This is an annual occurrence for the area, but the level of the floodwaters varies. Creeks running through the valley get clogged due to beaver activity, other material, and runoff. One creek runs underground through the back part of my property. It's a lush, beautiful valley when it isn't several feet underwater. The river is close by but is surrounded by large banks and old railroad berms.

By my third year on the property, my luck had run out.

The floodwaters came from what meteorologist called a perfect storm. There had been a major snowstorm that lasted for about a week. Snow is an annual occurrence here, but usually just a dusting once or twice during the season. Rarely does a snowstorm leave several feet of snow behind. The snow was deep, and the winds blew drifts to four feet high.

Potty breaks were an issue for all the dogs, except Lenny. A tall boy like Lenny had no problem leaping through the snow to find a place to take care of business. But it was during this snowstorm that Richard lost Lenny. I came home from work around midnight to find Richard walking around in the snow, calling Lenny's name. He had let Lenny out and then watched TV until he decided Lenny had been gone too long. The property was fenced but not gated. Richard was in a panic.

I didn't share his panic. I knew Lenny was close by, but I was glad that Richard loved Lenny so much the thought of losing him was distressing. I drove around and noticed there were no tracks in the snow. There had been no fresh snowfall in hours, so Lenny should have been easy to track, unless he took the paved roads. I called his name as I drove, sure that he could hear me. I had a feeling he was at the neighbor's house, because he liked to go exploring over there.

As I was driving down the gravel road next to her house, I turned and looked back at my house. There was Lenny, coming around the driveway and going up to the front door. This motivated Richard to put up gates at the driveway. Once this was done, Lenny was unable to wander off.

Another yearly weather phenomenon is the Pineapple Express—a sudden warming of weather accompanied by a voluminous amount of rain. One such rainstorm came when the snow stopped. With several feet of snow on the ground and in the mountains, the rains melted the snow at a rapid pace. Adding to the perfect storm was the positioning of the moon and the effect it had on the tides. Melting snow on the ground and in the mountains, lots of rain, and high tides meant there would be record flooding in the valley. When the river breaks its banks and floods the valley, it comes in fast but not as fast as flash flooding. It's a steady rising of the water level.

The dogs loved the flooded property. Ruby and Panzer took the opportunity to swim in the deeper pools of water. While the dogs frolicked in the water, stress was my constant companion. It was hard to tell when to leave the house. The property had flooded so many times before, but water had never come into the house.

When the water crept into the garage late at night, we decided we should leave. We put the dogs in a detached shop at a high point on the property and spent the night at a neighbor's house. The cats stayed in the house, because I thought they would go to high ground.

We fell asleep for a few short hours. In the early morning, the sound of a hovercraft on its way to rescue our neighbor Angela and her husband woke us.

We waited until the floodwaters receded enough for us to be able to get back into our home. It didn't take long, since the waters back out almost as fast as they come in. The shop didn't escape the floodwaters. When we went to check on the dogs, we discovered it had had a couple inches of water in it overnight. The dogs were happy to see us and the water had little if any affect on them. A few hours later, we were able to get back in the house and check the damage. The cats were stressed and happy we were home. The water had come in the house about six inches. That might not sound like much, but it meant lots of work was in our future.

The dogs didn't care. They were happy and stress-free. There was on-site swimming access, food, shelter, and bare ground for relieving themselves. It was all they needed. Shelter for us was now in the form of a borrowed fifth-wheel trailer. It didn't matter to the dogs that we were cramped together in this trailer while the house was rebuilt. I envied their no-stress approach to life. We had each other, and that was all we needed.

The remodeling process was a slow one; it took five months. When floodwaters enter a structure, they bring with it bacteria, decaying matter, and feces from the valley. The house had to be dried, floors removed, and sheet rock cut out. Then a layer of bleach was sprayed all over the exposed walls and floors.

There were many contractors at the house during this time. Richard was working days, and I went to work in the afternoon. Most of the contractors didn't mind the dogs, and the dogs didn't mind them. One contractor insisted the dogs not be around when he worked on the house. I put Cowboy and Lenny in a garden shed, which had been converted into a makeshift laundry room. Ruby and Panzer went to a kennel. We didn't know this kennel was sorely inadequate, despite being licensed.

Richard had asked for Ruby and Panzer to share a kennel, since being kenneled at a strange location would stress them. When Richard went to pick up the pair, he noticed Ruby was limping. He asked the staff what had happened. They said Panzer had chewed on Ruby's foot all day because he was stressed. It hadn't occurred to them to separate the two.

During this chaotic time, someone dumped off a black Labrador puppy at the river. I did everything I was supposed to do to try to locate her people. No one came forward to claim her. I named her Lucy, and she stayed with us for a few days in the trailer until we found her a home. It was a close call avoided; we'd almost had a fifth dog.

CHAPTER 7

Enter the Catalyst

Part of my job as a law enforcement officer is creating and maintaining relationships with partner organizations. On one of my networking trips, I unsuspectingly walked into a situation that would change me forever. I was on swing shift on a summer evening, and the sun was moving low. The temperature was still warm but starting to cool off. The building I was headed to was small and boxy. It shared a parking lot with the Tribal Fire Department. I parked my car and walked toward the building.

That was when I heard a horrific screeching sound coming from somewhere between the two buildings. I didn't immediately recognize the sound as a dog. The more I listened and looked around, the more I realized it was a dog, and I wondered if it was in serious distress or hurt.

I finally spotted a kennel. In it was a tiny black puppy. His feces-covered paws were up on the wire of the kennel, and he was trying desperately to get me to give him some much-needed attention. Not just his paws were full of feces. He had feces all over his fur. There was no water or food anywhere in the kennel.

My next order of business was to figure out why the poor pup was in the kennel. I walked into the office and asked my friend, who was the only one working. He told me the dog had been dropped off, and animal control had not been by to pick him up. The dog needed to be cleaned up and fed, and I insisted it happen immediately.

The pup was more than happy to be out of his kennel. He was black, but a matte black instead of shiny, which usually indicates poor nutrition. His hair was also thin in areas, and he smelled awful. I took him into the office and gave him a quick bath, which lifted his spirits. He didn't look much better, and he still had an odor about him. I thought he must have some kind of skin infection. When I placed him on the ground, he belly crawled across the floor like a marine sniper on a secret mission. The poor pup couldn't stop itching.

Business was handled, and I needed to be on my way. A large bowl of food and an oversized stuffed animal went in the kennel with the pup after we cleaned out the feces. The screeching started again. I made my friend promise to try to find the pup a home overnight, or I would pick him up the next day and take him to the shelter.

The following day, I called my friend to check on the dog. No, he hadn't had any luck finding a home. Yes, he tried, he really did. It was time to take matters into my own hands. The thought of the poor pup living in his feces with his infection, begging for human affection, was more than I could bear.

I called Richard and asked him to pick up the pup and take him to my vet. During the ride, something happened between him and the pup, which Richard didn't want to admit. The dog was starting to work his magic, slowly and stealthily. Maybe he was in training for a secret mission.

Later that evening, Richard called to tell me about the visit to the vet. The pup had demodectic mange and worms, but otherwise he was pretty healthy. Vet visits aren't cheap, especially for sick dogs. That visit cost three hundred dollars.

A few weeks of baths with a special medicated soap, and he would be as good as new. I received a picture of the pup after his first medicated bath. If dogs could smile, this one was smiling. He was in a sit, his ears were perked up, and his brows were pulled up. His eyes said to me, "How do you like me now?" Oh, and Richard had named him Moose—another victory for Moose and the unseen web he was spinning.

I learned that stray dogs with medical conditions are usually euthanized as opposed to being treated at shelters. Most people searching for a new pet aren't looking for one with special needs, so these animals are overlooked. Shelter expenses are high, and kennel space is at a premium. It is usually up to a rescuer to collect these animals and treat them before trying to find them homes.

Moose wouldn't be going to the shelter after all. His health issues would be taken care of while he stayed with us, and I looked for his forever home. Taking care of a dog with demodectic mange is easy. Medicated soap is used to bathe the dog. The soap sits on the dog for a specified time and then is washed off. The process is repeated on a prescribed schedule. The bugs causing the mange and then the hair loss would soon be gone. Growing back the hair would be a lengthier process.

I was lucky Moose was a puppy; I could get him to believe baths were fun. He was a fantastic patient when it came to baths. He was happy to be in the sink being loved on while he waited for the soap to work. Demodectic mange isn't contagious in dog-to-dog contact unless that contact is extended. The example the vet gave was a puppy catching it from its mother when it's suckling. But Richard insisted that Moose sleep in the garage to be on the safe side.

I would check on Moose every night when I came home from work. I would open the door, and tiny little Moose would get out of his bed to come and greet me. He would wag his tail and dutifully go back to his bed when he realized he hadn't talked me into taking him inside. He never made a fuss.

Moose's days of sleeping in the garage were few. I couldn't stand the thought of him being alone after all he had been through, so I made him a bed in our walk-in closet. I made sure he was comfortable, and he happily snuggled into his bed. That didn't last long either. It's an amazing feeling looking into the face of a sweet, grateful puppy and knowing one soul was saved from a horrible life. I wanted to snuggle with that sweetness.

Richard didn't want Moose in the bed, because Cowboy was already on the foot of the bed. He took up a good chunk of the bed, and dogs don't take your comfort into consideration. I would sneak Moose out of the closet and smuggle him into bed with me. From that day on, Moose has spent every night in my bed.

We did halfheartedly ask the neighbors if anyone wanted a puppy, as we didn't want the pack to become a five-member team. One of the neighbors knocked on our door after a few weeks and said he knew a woman looking for a dog, if Moose was still available. I looked at Richard, and he said, "No, we're going to keep him."

Oh, Moose, you are good.

CHAPTER 8

Spinning the Web

Moose and Cowboy were fast friends. Moose loved to run, jump, wrestle, and play. He found the perfect playmate in Cowboy, who had always been a puppy at heart. They truly enjoyed each other's company.

Occasionally the obnoxious puppy antics were too much even for Cowboy. After an extended play session, he would sit down, shoulders slumped and head slightly lowered. It was clear to me he was exhausted. Moose wasn't, and he didn't understand that the older dog was done. He continued to charge and bite at Cowboy. Frustrated, Cowboy would make several quick snaps at Moose, baring his teeth for emphasis. Moose still didn't understand, so I had to settle him down.

I couldn't help but laugh, because this was the only time Cowboy had ever lost his temper. I would let Cowboy know it was okay as I escorted the rambunctious pup to a toy or another pursuit besides irritating him. There was never a grudge held between those two. Through play, Cowboy was learning confidence and how to defend himself. Although the growls coming from him during play would scare a bear, he always had a soft mouth. It was always play with Moose.

Soon the magic started to happen. Lenny reacted to Moose with interest but kept his distance. He was still learning to trust;

his past experiences kept him from seeking interaction with the other dogs. He didn't approach Moose for friendship; Moose approached him. I watched as Moose shared his toys with Lenny. Lenny had never been shown such kindness before. My heart would melt when little Moose would lie next to giant Lenny, just enjoying the sunshine or passing off a toy. What I didn't know at the time was Moose wasn't a nurturer; he was a leader. He was evaluating every member of the pack. It was clear Lenny wasn't a threat, and if Moose wanted to lead him, Lenny surely would follow.

Lenny eventually trusted Moose, and finally Lenny started to act like a dog. He would chase Moose, and Moose would chase him. I have heard Lenny bark only one time. He was playing with Moose, and Moose got a bit too rambunctious. Lenny barked at him and made quick snaps of his jaw. I chuckled at this gentle giant correcting the overzealous little boy.

A while later, Lenny would chase Moose when I tossed Moose a ball. He would clumsily lope around Moose, cut him off, and run into him. Moose was always patient with Lenny and let him play with him, even though his sole focus was his ball. Moose seemed to have the glue needed to bring the pack together into a cohesive family.

The first time I saw Lenny gallop toward me without my calling his name, my heart skipped a beat. Lenny had changed, and it was obvious. A neighbor even mentioned how much he had changed. He was finally enjoying his life and just being a dog.

Lenny opened up in other ways as well. He loved chasing Moose around the yard so much he started teaching us humans this game. If he was feeling particularly energetic, he would gallop around us. I figured this meant he wanted to chase me. I would run in circles around a large cedar tree, and Lenny—with his long legs—would gallop behind or next to me. Once he got past me, I would smack him gently on the rear. Lenny would stop, spin around 180 degrees, and not let me near his behind again. We played this game as long as either of us had the wind for it.

Lenny also became more affectionate with Richard and me, and eventually with other humans. He wasn't an expressive dog. His face always remained the same. He almost never barked or uttered any other sounds. Most dogs use their ears, body language, and sounds to let humans or other animals know what they're thinking.

One day I was sitting next to him, stroking his head. He lifted his paw and gently placed it on my hand when I stopped. I began petting him again and stopped to see if he would remind me to pet him. He did.

Lenny was a favorite of guests. They would often sit next to him, admiring his size and gentle nature. He soon began asking them for affection in the same manner he'd taught me to give him more. Lenny didn't seek out affection very often. He remained a stoic, gentle giant of a dog.

Ruby was indifferent toward Moose, but she believed she was Moose's superior. One summer day when Moose was still very young, he and I were relaxing on the couch. The sun was shining in the window, and Moose was lying on my lap while I read a book. Ruby walked toward me, and Moose growled and bit my calf. I wondered what I had done to deserve that. He was looking at Ruby, but he bit me. It was a quick bite and painful, but he didn't break my skin or leave a bruise. A bit of misguided contempt, I thought. He was guarding me, and I knew I would need to learn to put a stop to that behavior.

Ruby and Moose fought only one other time. Ruby thought Moose had found some food in the grass, and she had her issues with food. She snapped at him, and Moose bit her once but hung on. She stood her ground and fought back. Ruby was sore, but the bite didn't tear her flesh.

Moose's reaction to being scolded was heartbreaking, but I stood firm. He sat in a perfect sit: feet pulled in tight, his ears pulled down, and not looking at me. The disappointment was clear on both our parts. I wasn't sure if he was upset that I was angry or if he was upset that he was baited into a fight.

I later learned this pose is how dogs send a message to calm down. I was upset, and I needed to calm down. Moose always sought to please me. The thought of his disenchantment with me broke my heart. Even I don't control my temper all the time, and I've regretted lashing out. Still, my job is to protect them, even if it's from themselves.

True to form, Panzer wasn't impressed with this little boy. He wanted to show Moose that he was the boss. Moose didn't appreciate his teaching style, the same one Panzer had used with Cowboy and Lenny. Moose wouldn't be bullied, and he wouldn't be attacked. He never started a fight with Panzer, but he sure would take on a fight and stay in it. Panzer was a bit hard-headed and didn't take his lessons quickly.

One afternoon, I came home from work and let the dogs out. We played and walked around the yard. The dogs had spent all day cooped up and needed to burn some energy. There's a large one-hundred-year-old birch tree on the side of my driveway. Moose was on to some scent in a hollow of the tree. Panzer wanted to take over the hunt, so he attacked Moose. The fight was on, and I had to break them apart. It happened so fast—about as fast as my temper escalated with Panzer. I hate dogfights, and Panzer was causing so many of them. Moose was a clench biter. He bit and hung on, not releasing until he was ready. Panzer bit and shook, which usually caused tearing of flesh. I reacted quickly enough that there was no physical damage—this time.

Something needed to change—and fast. I was still having trouble finding the resources I needed. Moose was getting along great with all the dogs, except Panzer. He never started any issues within the pack. He was beginning to become the leader, whether or not any of the dogs liked it.

CHAPTER 9

Moose's Aversions

For the most part, Moose was a happy, energetic, rambunctious dog. During his first two years, his personality was growing and changing. I was ill-prepared for the powerful, strong-willed, independent, loving dog that was Moose.

Other than the incident with Ruby, Moose bit me one other time. I had a rag that I was trying to keep away from him. I was moving it from hand to hand, trying to keep it out of his grasp. Finally, I held the rag over my head, and Moose accepted the challenge. He jumped up, and while staring at the rag, he bit me in the chest. There was no damage, no broken skin, but it hurt.

I rolled Moose onto his back and pinned him there. The look of terror in his eyes made me recoil. I released him right away. I was horrified. Moose got up and ran off to play with his pack mates. He had forgiven me, but would he trust me again? I had made a grievous mistake that ate at me for years. Moose was over it right away.

I decided it was time to take Moose to the vet and have him neutered. My vet had told me there was no rush to neuter him during his first year of life. He was then about six months old, too soon by some standards, but I needed help with that budding powerhouse. I planned on neutering him sooner or later, but for some reason I felt guilty deciding it was time. It didn't feel right. It felt like punishment, but I knew it would help manage Moose's behavior issues.

It was fast becoming clear Moose wasn't a fan of other dogs. My first clue was at the vet's office when I took him in for puppy shots. I had him on a leash, and his collar had a cheap plastic clasp. A tall, thin, middle-aged man with dark-brown hair walked in with his small dog as I was standing at the counter with my back to the door. Moose charged at the dog, breaking the clasp on his collar. He stopped and did nothing more before I recovered him. The owner of the other dog glared at me, perhaps wondering why I didn't have control of my crazy dog. The truth was, I was startled and puzzled by Moose's reaction. Though he was just a few months old, those collars were no match for his strength. I had to find collars with metal buckles.

At the house, we now had a gate at the entrance to the driveway. The entire property was reinforced with invisible fencing. A determined dog could still take the shock if it wanted to go after something on the other side. The gate was a huge help for keeping my dogs on my property and other animals off my property. Richard and I had been working on putting up welded-wire fencing over the barbed-wire fencing surrounding the property. With the right prompting or a break in a wire, the dogs were willing to duck under the barbed wire to chase or explore. Welded-wire fencing kept the dogs from being able to escape.

On a spring afternoon in early April, Richard and I were working on the last section of fencing. The day was unusual in that it was free of rain, making it a good day to work on fencing. There were Angus cattle grazing near the fence. The bulls especially have quite a bit of heft and are prone to having less-than-friendly temperaments. The young cattle were curious about what we were up to, but cautious. Angus aren't bottle reared like their Jersey milk cow cousins, making them a little leery of humans.

Moose was several months old by then. He was the only one of the dogs in the pasture with Richard and me. (He liked to stay close to his humans.) A young bull had come to the fence near where Richard and I were working. I had no idea Moose would be willing to take on an animal several times his size, but he did; he charged that bull. The invisible fence stopped him. We were fast behind him. I looked at the bull, and his eyes were wide in shock as he stared at Moose. The poor bull was terrified. If Moose had made it through the fence into the herd of cattle, they would likely have killed him. Also, in our state, livestock owners are allowed to shoot dogs that go after their herd. If the livestock owner doesn't get to the dog first, the county will take it and have it put down. I added cattle to the list of animals Moose didn't like.

Summer is the most beautiful time of the year in the Northwest. Some would say it's spring, with all its blooming flowers and trees. For me, it's summer, with the clear blue skies, tolerable temperatures, and daylight that extends far into the evening.

I put my vegetable garden next to my fence, because I thought the invisible fencing would deter garden varmints, such as my dogs. There was also a horse that grazed near my garden. It would come to the fence when I was working there and nibble the grass along the fence while I worked. I would greet it, and it would glance at me every once in a while until finally I pulled carrots for it and scratched its head.

On a beautiful summer evening when Moose wasn't quite two, I was working in my garden. The horse had come to visit and gotten scratches and carrots. After eating my carrots, the horse dropped its head over the fence near where I was working and grazed on my side of the fence. I stayed in the fenced and gated garden area and tended to the rest of my vegetables. My dogs were peacefully lounging—or so I thought.

I looked up and saw Moose staring at the horse and bearing down in what I knew to be a pre-pounce position. There was no growling, no warning issued whatsoever, but I knew his intent. I yelled, "No!" and began to work my way out of my garden. Moose glanced at me when I yelled. I swear he was entertained by my disapproval and was challenging me to catch him if I could. The horse was oblivious until Moose was eye to eye with it as he was cresting the fence. I kept yelling no as I ran to get Moose.

The horse had run away and was the only one listening to me as I yelled. It stopped running and faced us, Moose on the other side of the fence and me at the fence, ready to go over it to get him. I could see the horse had recovered and realized that a little pipsqueak of a dog was what had come over the fence. It pulled itself up, elongated its neck, and flared its nostrils.

Moose and I now saw a much bigger horse, a tall, indignant horse. I panicked and flew into action. I had a short window of time to save my crazy dog, and I had the obstacle of a fence. Moose was also in a panic. He was panting heavily and frantically pulling at the fence to try to make a hole. I started pulling up the bottom of the fence to make a hole for him to get back to safety. He no longer had the confidence or the ground room to take a running start at the fence to get over the top. I managed to make a big enough hole, and he gladly took the shock from the invisible fence to get back home.

Since he was now safely home, Moose carried on like nothing had happened. He went about playing with the other dogs. Once the interloper was off its property, the horse came back to the fence, and I apologized to it. I even pulled another carrot for it. I was relieved all was well, but I was mad at Moose for his antics. Yet I was secretly amused with his bravado at the same time. Horses were now added to the list of animals Moose didn't like.

I decided it was time for formal training. I believed Moose had pit bull in him, but not because I knew anything about the breed. People had commented that he looked like a pit bull. His dislike of dogs and other animals as well as his bite style seemed to point in that direction too. It's hard to find a good trainer and particularly for a dog with pit bull in his lineage. I tried a few trainers that were awful. It seemed as if their only training was reading a book and charging offensive amounts to "train" a dog.

I shared my concerns about Moose's behavior with a trainer. I told him about his issues and the thought he may be part pit bull and part Labrador. He told me I should put him down, because pit bulls are dangerous and can never have the aggressiveness trained out of them. I was angry and offended. I couldn't believe he had the nerve to tell me to kill my dog without even having met him. True to a dog's nature, Moose would have been kind and loving to her. My search for a trainer went on.

Not all of Moose's aversions were dangerous. Whenever my dogs have intestinal distress, the standard advice from the vet's office is to give them a bland diet. One time when Moose had diarrhea, I put him on chicken and rice. I cooked both and allowed them to cool a bit before I served them, since the rest of my dogs don't mind warm food. I placed the bowl down in front of Moose, and though he was quite hungry, he pulled his head back, furrowed his brow, and slowly backed away from the bowl. I picked it up and felt the food. It was a bit warm but not hot.

I made a show of blowing on the rice and fanning it with my hand, trying to get it to cool down a bit. The ever-vigilant Moose watched me blow on his food, and I hoped he was convinced. I placed it in front of him again. He again furrowed his brow, but this time, he barked at his food. I couldn't contain my laughter as I realized he was mimicking my actions the only way a dog could. After a few barks, the food was cool enough for him to eat.

Moose was such a fearless dog, it was hard for me to believe he had any fears. But I started to notice he wasn't willing to walk in certain parts of the house. His trouble areas were from the hallway into my bedroom, through the mudroom, and through living room to the front door. He would hang his head and creep forward until I went to him. I would put my hand on his back and walk with him. He would walk fast into the room with me by his side. I began to wonder if he was having vision problems. The hallways and mudroom were unlit most of the time, and those areas seemed to be giving him the most trouble.

I took Moose to his vet, who examined him and didn't find any issues. But he noticed Moose did seem fearful and hung his head. He recommended I take Moose to an eye specialist. I made an appointment for him.

The eye specialist's office was in a major city on a busy road. The office was small and surrounded by windows. I was early, so I sat in the truck with Moose. Once they opened, I went in the office without him. The receptionist was a young, friendly, heavyset blonde. I explained to her I had Moose with me, but he was animal-aggressive, and I would need help getting him into the office without issues. People were coming in with their dogs, and she understood. She asked me to wait in my truck and told me someone would come get me when it was time.

When the doctor was ready, I watched the tech move people to the far ends of the reception area. She was tall, dark-haired, and had a friendly smile as she waved at me to come in.

I got Moose out of the truck and walked to the office. He was always up for an adventure and was happy to walk with me. Once in the reception area, we walked fast toward the room where he was to see the specialist. Suddenly Moose stopped and spread all his limbs out, trying to keep from crossing the threshold. The lights were dim in the office, and I asked the tech to turn them up. After she did, Moose crossed the threshold with me using slow steps and great caution.

He calmed down as we waited for the vet. The doctor was a tall, middle-aged man with brown hair and glasses. He was kind and sat on the floor with Moose and me. Moose took to him right away. The doctor performed some tests and told me there was nothing wrong with Moose's vision. He had seen Moose standing at the closed door with his head dropped down and said he thought that was indicative of neck or back pain. He also thought it was an expression of fear, but not because Moose was having problems seeing. He said he would call Moose's regular vet and discuss his findings with him.

A friend asked me what kind of floors I had. I told her hardwood. She thought that maybe Moose was afraid of the floors. So I tested her theory. In my house, I placed carpets at the front door, in the mudroom, and in the hallways. It worked like magic. Moose had no problems with crossing those areas with carpeting. I was surprised, because the floors had always been hardwood. I figured he must have slipped and hurt himself one time when I wasn't aware. At least that aversion was easy to solve.

CHAPTER 10

The Training Begins

Lenny, Cowboy, and Ruby were pretty easy to manage. I never bothered teaching Lenny any commands. He never gave me any problems, so I didn't see the need. He had one speed: slow. He wasn't pushy, and he would come when I called. He was just easy to handle. Lenny would bristle when voices were raised, and he pulled away if I made sudden moves. I'm not sure what his previous life was like, and I'm glad I don't know.

Cowboy had the same easygoing manner. His biggest issue was his fear of people, which I just had to accept. He did learn basic commands, even though he pretended to be hard of hearing. Every command had to be given to him at least twice, and he would quickly break the command to do what he wanted to do.

In teaching Cowboy how to do a simple sit, it became clear he had structural issues with his knees. His behind couldn't reach the ground when he tried to sit. He would have to sit on one cheek or the other and kick out a leg to sit comfortably. This made training him to sit difficult. Richard and I joked that Cowboy was our million-dollar dog; he tore his anterior cruciate ligament at a couple of years old, and the fix was an expensive surgery.

A few years later, Cowboy suffered an autoimmune disease

called trigeminal neuralgia. One Sunday, I noticed his mouth was hanging open for hours. He was a mouth breather, but this was a bit excessive, even for him. He wasn't eating or drinking. I called the emergency clinic and was told he had to come in immediately. Trigeminal neuralgia is painful. In dogs, the nerves on both sides of the jaws are attacked, and the dog can't close its mouth. This means it can't get food or water without help.

Cowboy spent the night in the emergency clinic, getting rehydrated before being sent to a neurologist. This again was an expensive excursion. I also had to hand feed and water Cowboy for about a week. He hated it as much as I did. He was hungry and would make a mess trying to scarf down his food. I had to give him water through a giant syringe. He didn't take well to this procedure and insisted on attempting to drink on his own. One week and a couple of thousand dollars later, Cowboy was back to himself. The only upside was he would never have to go through this again. Trigeminal neuralgia never comes back.

Ruby came to me with basic training skills. She did have an issue about food aggression, which hadn't come to light with her previous owner, since she was the only dog in that house. And of course there was her issue with female dogs. Ruby never even waited for food or ate treats while other dogs were around. So Panzer, Lenny, and Ruby all ate in their own rooms. This was an easy way to manage dinnertime and worked out well.

Panzer was the first training hurdle I tackled. He was my biggest challenge. He has always had anxiety issues. In basic behavior training, he tried not to pay attention. He would climb on me or lick me, whine and pace around. Other times he would ignore my instructions and scratch himself or even throw himself on the ground and expose his belly. If I tried to ignore his antics, he would bark at me. Panzer was unsure of himself. I needed to build his confidence in himself and my confidence in me.

My vet recommended a pair of trainers, Brigit and Jerrell. The pair said their specialty was training difficult and aggressive dogs. After a brief phone consultation, I had an appointment to start training with Panzer. The trainers liked to use Schutzhund techniques, the type used to train police dogs. They seemed to be capable of handling aggressive dogs, and their fees reflected that. I knew I wouldn't be able to afford much training, but I had to start somewhere.

The trainers' property was completely fenced and gated. Trees and several outbuildings dotted the landscape. A large riding barn was the building where we would be doing our training. In the barn, I was briefed on the training process. We discussed basics on how the mind of a dog works and what a dog needs from us in a leader. During the discussion, Brigit interrupted Jerrell and asked me if I realized how bonded Panzer was to me. I didn't, and I was surprised she saw it in him. She told me to look at him. Panzer was glued to my side and was looking up at me expectantly. She told me he was looking to me for guidance and was willing to please me. I'm embarrassed to confess I'd never noticed his attachment.

After working on basic training, we began to work on confidence building. There was an A-frame in the barn like the ones used in agility competitions. It took a few tries, but Panzer conquered the A-frame like a champ. He ended up loving the A-frame so much that we built him one at the house. Soon he was running the frame up one side and down the other. His favorite part of running the frame was stopping at the top and demanding attention. He would look down at me with his ears flopping forward and bark until I petted him. He was king of the A-frame. It was a start, but we had much more work to do.

Moose was the next to head off to train with Brigit and Jerrell. These two didn't buy into the hysteria against the pit bull breed. They loved pit bulls and found them to be smart and easy to train. They had no fear of dealing with Moose or his issues.

Brigit and Jerrell wouldn't go to people's homes without an extra fee that was far more than what I was able to afford. The problem now was getting there. As Moose grew, he became terrified of vehicles. When I took him to the vet, I would place him in the back seat of my truck. He would begin pacing and panting, and I could see the whites of his eyes. I didn't know how I was going to make it to the trainers without causing him way too much stress.

At the time, I didn't know how Moose's life had started. I later learned that he'd been put in a garbage bag and tossed out of a moving truck. A woman following the driver saw movement and thought a baby was in the bag. She stopped to investigate and discovered Moose. She took Moose to the police department and left him in their care. Thankfully, there was a guardian angel driving behind that truck. If she hadn't stopped, Moose would have died a tragic death. Had I known this story beforehand, I would have understood the source of his anxiety.

I told Brigit about Moose's anxiety in vehicles. She told me to place him in the truck, start it, and just sit there. I was to go about my business, checking e-mails or whatever I needed to do, and also talk to Moose in a relaxed, happy tone. The point was to make it casual and seem like it was no big deal. I tried this, and Moose panted, but he didn't panic.

The next step was to take short drives around the driveway, then longer and longer trips. It worked. Moose liked the front seat better than the back seat, and he soon loved to ride in cars. The transition was so complete, he would jump in visitors' cars, move to the passenger seat, and wait to be taken on a ride. I was impressed with Brigit's knowledge and ease in solving a problem that had baffled me.

The trainers liked Moose. Brigit particularly loved his unique coloring. In the sunshine, Moose's undercoat was highlighted, revealing that his fur wasn't completely black. Rather it had a beautiful mahogany undertone. He was eager to learn and learned fast. He also had a charming head tilt when he would sit calmly and listen for instructions.

They also noticed that Moose had a high prey drive. He had a laser-like focus when "prey," such as a ball or a stuffed animal on a rope, was presented to him. He pounced and chased after these prey and wanted to do it over and over again. My homework was to burn off his youthful energy by giving him something to chase, such as a ball. I had played ball with Moose, but I discovered it was fun for him to keep the ball away from me once he had his fill of chasing it. Jerrell taught me how to get Moose to drop the ball for me.

As we sat talking after a long play session, we talked about what constitutes a "good" dog. Brigit told me she believes a good dog is a well-trained dog that has a skill and exceeds at that skill. A great dog can control his or her passion or prey drive and bring it out on command.

While we were talking, Moose was tearing apart the tennis ball he had been playing with. The curious thing about his destruction was that he first removed the elastic banding around it. We laughed at the intellectual debanding of the ball. Moose was trainable and enjoyed training sessions, but we also had much more work to do. The need to burn off energy was just one facet of Moose's personality.

I didn't feel like I had a handle on training, and I didn't feel like I understood the inner workings of a dog's mind. I especially didn't know how to handle an intelligent, high prey drive in a determined but sweet dog like Moose. All those issues seemed to come to a head when he was about eighteen months of age. I now had a complex powerhouse of a teenager on my hands. He took every bit of my attention, patience, and training time.

Moose had always been soft on Lenny. One beautiful spring afternoon, all six of us were outside on the front part of the wraparound deck. The dogs were lounging, and I was sitting on my porch swing with my laptop on my lap. Lenny wanted to pass from the side deck, crossing in front of us to go back in the house. Moose jumped up, lunged at him, and snarled. He wasn't going to grant passage.

Lenny held his ground, not even phased. I jumped up off the porch swing, causing my laptop to hit the porch, and yelled at Moose to calm down. Of course, Moose looked at me with raised eyebrows as if asking, "Who really needs to calm down here?" He was setting the ground rules on who was the boss. I didn't get the memo. I didn't care for Moose's rule-setting methods because I didn't know when the lessons were coming.

I lacked so much confidence and skill, so I kept in contact with Brigit about Moose's behavior. She mentioned the option of training Moose to be a bomb-sniffing dog. A local company had a program where they accepted dogs to work for them. This meant I would have to donate Moose to his handler. He would have to live and work with the person who would train him.

I checked into it only because I wanted Moose to be a balanced and happy dog. If that meant I wasn't the best person for him, I thought I could live with that, as long as he was happy. The program was looking for dogs, but one important trait they looked for was the ability to be around other dogs. They weren't looking for dog-aggressive dogs. This wasn't going to be the program for Moose. In hindsight, I'm grateful I didn't have the opportunity to rehome him.

Moose may not have appreciated other four-legged creatures, but he adored the two-legged variety. The only training I had to do with Moose and people was to stop him from jumping on them. When people came to visit, he would become excited. He would jump up, place his paws on the visitor's stomach or chest, and throw his weight into them. I called it center punching. He would almost knock people over. It was a dangerous display of affection I put a stop to without dampening his love of people.

Moose made people smile, especially me. His antics were showstoppers. He didn't like to swim, but he loved sprinklers and a wading pool. I purchased sprinklers that are on a long stake and swirl around, spreading water in a large circle. Moose loved those sprinklers. He would stand on his hind legs and try to catch as much of the water as possible in his mouth. On his hind legs, he was as tall as the sprinkler, and he would rise up onto his toes to try to reach the water that was shooting above.

There is a road that runs along the front of my property. Just past my property is an access to the river. In the summertime, this road has heavy traffic. On a hot, beautiful Northwest summer day, my flowerbeds were parched. I was watering a bed about seventy feet from the road. As always, Moose followed me around the yard as I worked. When he heard the sprinkler come on, he began his two-legged sprinkler dance. Up on his toes he went, stretching and hopping with an open mouth, trying to capture as much water as possible.

I heard a hearty chortle coming from the road. There was a large man wearing a sleeveless T-shirt and a black leather vest. A female rider sat on the back of his motorcycle. They were heading toward the river but stopped when they saw the two-legged dance and had a good and laugh at Moose's antics. That was my boy, a crowd pleaser. And Moose wasn't phased. He had no idea he was entertaining. He just wanted to conquer the water.

Moose loved the attention people gave him. He would soak it up and move in for a pet when people came toward him, smiling and speaking nicely to him. I believed if Moose were a service dog, it would be a great way to share his comical personality with people who need to smile. Having Moose go to a hospital or nursing home and letting him work his magic on people sounded like a perfect plan for him, so I began researching what it took for a dog to be a certified therapy dog.

There's much more work to having a therapy dog than just throwing a vest on the dog. For a dog to become a certified service dog, it must first pass the Canine Good Citizen certification. It didn't seem like it would be hard for Moose to pass the test at all. He wasn't food aggressive, and he loved children and followed commands. But there was a catch: he had to be able to ignore other dogs in his immediate area.

Moose just wasn't able to ignore other dogs. They incensed him. He would lung and bark at dogs when riding in the truck. He would also charge the fence if there were dogs on the road next to the house. I had no idea why he had a great dislike for other dogs and animals. It was a curiosity to me that he got along so well with his own pack but despised any dog outside the fence. For the time being, the ball was going to have to be the best outlet for Moose's energy.

CHAPTER 11

Working It Out

Life is rarely peaceful when you have five dogs. We were still sorting out issues within the pack. I hadn't given up looking for a trainer that could help me with my unique situation, and my search was extensive. I was surprised by how few people put time and money into training their dogs. No one could offer me a recommendation. Finally, I found the trainers we needed. This couple was everything I could hope for. These two worked miracles.

Tommy and Corday had recently moved to the state and started their training business, the Evergreen School For Dogs. They were new to the state, but in no way were they new to training. (Richard wanted nothing to do with the training and refused to participate.)

We started with a consultation meeting where they met my dogs, and I briefed them on the issues we were having. Just in that short time, I could tell these two were different. They were knowledgeable and didn't give me canned answers to my questions. It was a comfort to hear they had no prejudices about certain breeds. They had trained many difficult dogs, and they didn't shy away from a challenge.

The best part about the training was them being willing to come to my house, which is what I needed. It wasn't enough to attempt to train each dog individually. I needed someone to come to the house and see what the pack dynamic was like as well as the issues with loose dogs roaming the neighborhood. Most important, they gave me hope.

Tommy and Corday start the training process together. They were a younger couple. Corday was tall, thin, with long, flowing brown hair, big eyes, and a warm smile. Tommy was also tall and thin with dark hair and a boyish face. They were a harmonious couple and worked well together. Both of them had a calm energy and a knack for reading my dogs' behavior. Tommy had a seriousness about him that was part concentration and part evaluation. Each came with their own brand of magic in their bag of tricks.

We started our training with some basics: working on recall, working on stays and downs. Those are easy enough when you have one dog; when you have five dogs, things can get a bit chaotic. As Tommy worked on training my dogs and me, it was obvious the dogs were the better students. Trying to get more than one dogs to do what you want at the same time is a monstrous undertaking. Lenny, my oldest dog, missed out on training because he rarely got off the couch and had no interest in the sessions.

My trainers never became angry, yelled, or panicked. If my dogs got into a fight with each other, I did it all. I yelled, got angry, and panicked. It's no wonder I wasn't getting anywhere.

Tommy would just assess the situation and then handle it.

I was amazed at how fast answers came to him. It was like I could see him thinking. He could tell me how to respond to any situation and any behavior. I didn't trust myself, and I didn't trust my dogs, but I did trust my trainers. With easy explanations, they were able to start me on a path of understanding and then of changing the undesirable behavior.

Training was going well, but I still didn't have a complete understanding of Moose's temperament. He had always been curious about my cats but stayed away from them. I had given Dude, the friendly male stray that walked into my home, to my neighbor, because he lacked a healthy fear of dogs. My female cats stayed away from the dogs and had no interest in interacting with them.

Another storm came thirteen months after the flood that forced me to remodel my home. This time we didn't evacuate. We were in the house when the water came in. All five dogs, Richard, and I sat on the bed. The cats were on high ground in a spare room. We watched as the waters came in the house and rose to the level of the baseboard, which is about two inches.

Those two inches were enough to warrant another remodel of the house. Floors had to be torn out, walls cut out, and so much more. The thought of another remodel stressed me. I didn't want to go through the process again. The waters receded at a rapid pace, as they always do. The flood left me with a dirty house, five bored dogs, and a husband who had to leave the state for work.

The next day, the cleanup had to start. I packed up the cats and asked Angela to keep them until I could get the house somewhat redone. The doors had all been removed and put in the shop to dry out. I had a friend help me with the remodel, and we did almost all the work ourselves. Four months earlier, I'd had surgery on my foot for plantar fasciitis. I was standing on my feet most of the days, installing floors and other woodwork, along with all the other aspects of remodeling a flooded house. Needless to say, I didn't heal like I should, and I was in severe pain. The pain was so bad I had to buy a cane just to get around. I was exhausted and at my wit's end.

I went back to work after two weeks but continued to work on the house every night. I became worried about my cats, because Angela's cats had fleas, and a few of them had tapeworms. Of course, I didn't want my cats to get sick, and I had her bring my cats back to my house. Angela and I set up a special baby gate made for pets at the door to a room that they spent most of their time in. The gate had a small door at the bottom that allowed the cats to go through.

We let the cats out in the room. Before I could shut the small door, Sugar walked out into the pack of four dogs curiously watching the return of the cats. I had moved to grab her when she decided to run to my bedroom. Moose gave chase. I frantically tried to catch her, but there were no doors to shut. In her confusion, Sugar ran into my walk-in closet then back into my bedroom. Moose was quicker than I was and grabbed her around the chest and shook her. I finally got him to release her, but it was too late. He didn't make any puncture wounds, but it didn't take long for Sugar to pass, perhaps of a heart attack.

Angela and I packed Harleigh Ann up, and she went to live permanently in Angela's house. Angela's husband buried Sugar for me on their property so she wouldn't be disturbed in her rest. I'd thought I was at my wit's end before, but I learned I didn't know where the end was. I was devastated.

I was also angry at Moose, but he didn't understand why. To him, Sugar was just another prey animal, and it was his job to chase it and kill it. He didn't understand this was a pet, a cat that I loved and that had been part of my life for sixteen years. When Moose knew he'd done something wrong, he'd sit with his feet pulled in close, ears pulled low, and eyes diverted. But he stood and looked at me, his eyebrows pulled up, mouth hanging open, panting, and then walked off.

My brother happened to call me a few hours after this incident. We had never been close; we spent more time at odds with each other than we did in harmony. This was one of the rare good times. I told him what happened, and he immediately thought Moose was a bad dog. I found myself defending Moose. I explained to him that my cat was no different to him than a rabbit or other prey animal. He understood what I was saying and told me he was proud of me for being strong and managing it all on my own. Moose had pulled some good out of the situation after all.

  I contacted Tommy and updated him on what had happened. He agreed that cats weren't compatible with Moose, and Moose wasn't to blame for his actions. I had so much more to learn about managing Moose's personality.

CHAPTER 12

My Breaking Point

Moose was getting adept at jumping the primitive four-foot fence surrounding the property. I wasn't getting any younger and will never get faster. One time he jumped the fence, caught the edge of a barb, and sliced straight down his male part. It didn't faze him in the least.

On a beautiful summer afternoon, I was watering my flowerbeds while the dogs were lounging in the grass. All peace ended abruptly when a stray dog walked down the road. Moose took notice when the dog, a large mixed-breed, stopped at the edge of the property. It was looking down the road at another loose dog, which had come out to the street and was confronting it. I yelled at Moose as I dropped the water and headed toward him. I was too slow. He cleared the fence.

I quickly climbed over the barbed-wire fence before there was any damage done. When I got over the fence, I grabbed an infuriated Moose by the collar. The other dog was incensed as well. I knew what Moose could do, but I didn't know what the other dog could do. Fortunately, it ended well—that time.

This incident pushed me over the edge. I was doing everything in my power to keep Moose under control, and I didn't want to fail him. One doesn't have to look hard to find many stories about dogs that bite people or other animals. The sentence is almost always death. This is especially true if the dog is of a "dangerous" breed, such as a pit bull.

I immediately made two phone calls. The first was to my landscaper. I cried, and I begged him to come over the next day and put up a six-foot fence around the part of my property that faced the road. God bless him; he dropped everything he was doing the next day to come to my rescue. He is a great man with a huge heart, and I will always be indebted to him.

The next phone call was to my trainers. I was in tears with them too. I couldn't fail my dog. I would never forgive myself if Moose were taken away from me because I didn't do everything in my power for him. They also agreed to come over and do some intensive training with us the upcoming weekend, after the new fence was erected. I could breathe again.

Dogs aren't capable of having rational thoughts. We can't predict their every move or when a trigger will sneak up on them. But it's our job to be ready and to protect them from the consequences of their shortsightedness. This is unconditional love. I didn't like Moose's behavior, but I loved him. And I needed to help him get to a place of balance and peace. It was gut-wrenching and exhausting but worth it in the long run.

Part of our training included my trainer's wife bringing a dog to the fence. My job was to recall Moose and regain control of him. This went pretty well as long as none of the other dogs were out with Moose. He didn't try to clear or charge the fence, and he would come back to me after a few tries. Once the other dogs were reintroduced, this became a daunting task. When a dog gets around its pack, and they all decide it's a good idea to bark and charge the fence, it's hard to try to break them of that. In time, Moose was the one that always came running back to me when I called him.

After we learned some basic commands and skills, my trainer thought we could try walking Moose with one of their dogs. I didn't like the idea of getting Moose within striking distance of another dog. Tommy must have sensed my fear or just knew better, but either way, he said he would walk Moose.

Corday would walk their dog, an older, passive female dog. We began the walk out on the road, and it was going well. The female dog was out of striking range but walking near Moose. We walked for a short distance then stopped and talked. Moose was behaving well, and I was beginning to relax.

Corday suggested that we let Moose sniff the female's behind. Moose sniffed and then in a split second I saw a subtle change. He stopped moving. I had just started to warn them when Moose nipped the poor girl in the behind. Tommy and Corday reacted fast, and no damage was done—except to my confidence. To say I felt horrible would be an understatement.

Tommy suggested we take Moose out of his comfort zone, his domain, his property, by walking him walking at their place. The thought was to see if Moose was less confident and confrontational when he was on another dog's territory. I was willing to give anything a shot. A week or so later, I drove Moose to their property.

I didn't have a muzzle yet for Moose, so they provided me with a metal basket muzzle, which is like a cage that fits over the dog's snout. It allows for panting and even room to accept treats. Once again I wasn't going to be the one walking Moose. The stress was unbearable.

With the muzzle in place, my trainer's wife brought out the big dog. And I do mean that literally. He was a big, black German shepherd with confidence and attitude to match Moose's. That dog barked at Moose and let him know he didn't like him on *his* turf. Moose wasn't the kind of dog to give warnings by barking. He was the strong, silent type. Just as we were about to start the walk, Moose stopped, brought both of his paws to the muzzle, and pulled it off his face. We recovered, put the muzzle back on, and went for a brief walk.

It went well. The shepherd was calm and didn't cause any problems. Moose walked stiffly, alert and ready to go to combat if it became necessary. Of course, we wouldn't have allowed a confrontation. Back at the house, with the shepherd put away, Moose's muzzle was removed, and he was given some ball time.

He eased into his carefree attitude and chased the ball until he was tired.

My trainer told me he believed Moose would never get along with other dogs. He said Moose liked to fight and was a confident fighter. It broke my heart not to be able to share Moose with the world as a therapy dog.

But one morning Moose proved to me it should have been his calling. My neighbor Angela's daughter had cancer and was going for treatments twice a week. I offered to take her on one of those days, since it happened to fall on my day off, and I figured Angela could use a break. I loaded Moose into the front seat of my truck and picked up the patient. When she got in the truck, Moose crawled into her lap and licked her face. He continued to do so all the way to the hospital and all the way back. Moose made her laugh and forget about her problems for a few minutes.

I didn't understand why Moose got along so well in the pack if he didn't like other animals. He was the glue in our pack; he adjusted his contact with all the dogs according to their unique personalities. My trainer explained that since Moose was the last dog in the pack, and he came into the pack as a puppy, he accepted them as his family. He further explained this isn't an uncommon phenomenon. Moose's personality was being revealed to me in layers. Some layers made me cry, some frustrated me, some taught me lessons, and some made me laugh. But at the center was a dog that gave me more joy and love than I had ever known.

There is a school of thought that says there are no bad dogs, only bad owners. Or even worse, bad dogs aren't born; they are raised. I beg to differ. First, Moose is not a bad dog. He is a great dog that happens to not like other animals. Panzer is a good dog that is nervous by nature. There are people who are anxious because of the chemistry in their brain. I've never beat my dogs, abused them, tortured them, forced them to fight, left them chained to anything, or let them go hungry. I'm not a bad owner. I don't have bad dogs. I have dogs. Dogs are as different from each other as people are different from each other. Yes, tortured and abused dogs can turn into defensive dogs. I don't deny there's a correlation between the treatment of an animal and its behavior. But I believe a dog must have been abused to be a timid dog, a dog-aggressive dog, or a nervous dog.

Once I became familiar with dog-aggressive personalities, I grew more and more comfortable with pit bulls. In fact, I became somewhat of an advocate. I dispelled myths among people I talked to in my circles. I shared pit bulls needing adoption on my Facebook page. I even supported rescues any way I could, especially when they broke up dog-fighting rings.

The one thing I could never stomach was to be a part of an investigation of a dog-fighting ring. It seems every week there's a report of a ring being broken up. I keep hoping there will be an end to the torture. Every time I hear of the suffering, a piece of my soul is crushed. I despise everything about dog fighting and the people that torture dogs for profit.

Fighters keep these dogs out in the elements or in cages in cold, dark basements. The ground around where the dogs are staked with heavy chains is bare and muddy from their pacing. Often these heavy chains cause deformities in the dogs. Their elbows bend outward to take the pressure off their joints. It's a permanent disfigurement called chain-broken. If they're given shelter, it's usually in the form of a barrel or a primitive box. They're fed and watered on an infrequent basis. Loving human contact is out of the question.

The females are forced to produce litter after litter. They are often restrained in a rape stand so they cannot attack the breeder. Once they've fulfilled their usefulness, the fighters throw them in the pen to die as bait dogs or discard them on the streets. The gentle dogs are used for bait. The losers are often beaten, hung, or electrocuted to death. It's a disgusting world that I wish I could somehow help put an end to. If dogs are lucky enough to be rescued, most maintain their love for humans. How they still find us worthy of love is beyond my imagination.

Moose taught me these dogs are worthy of love,

companionship, and protection. They aren't worthy of contempt, torture, and death.

I'm a work in progress, as is my pack. Looking out for my dogs and providing safety and comfort for them is my top priority. Dogs labeled "dangerous" are usually killed at the shelters, and this always weighs heavily on my mind. Many cities honor breed-specific legislation. This means if a dog has a specific look, its owner must move or relinquish the dog to be killed.

This frightened me and caused me sleepless, tearful nights. I had to protect Moose; he was my friend, my loyal companion, and I owed him. Many dogs get the label "pit bull" based only on looks. People put these dogs into this category based not on fact but on fear and ignorance. I decided I needed more information in my armory, and the way to get it was to have my dogs' DNA tested.

CHAPTER 13

What Kind of Dog Is That?

I wanted to have proof of Moose's breed in case I was ever challenged or Moose ended up at the shelter. One by one, I had each of my dog's DNA tested. I purchased the kits on the Internet, and the process was simple. The kit contained two small brushes, which I swirled around inside the dog's cheek. I submitted the swabs, and the results showed up via e-mail a few days later. These days, they have DNA kits for humans too. We can learn our lineage and so much more through the swabbing of a cheek.

The results were surprising. Of all my dogs, I had guessed right on only two. I decided to have some fun with the process. I posted a picture of my dogs on Facebook and found out which of my friends were better at guessing breeds than I was. Breed knowledge isn't my strength.

The first dog I tested was Moose. It was an agonizing wait for the results. Of all my dogs, he had the cleanest bloodlines. He was composed of only two breeds. The first was obvious to me: he was half Labrador retriever. His boundless energy, his prey drive, his wavy back hair, and his soft facial features were all indicative of the breed. What came as a surprise to me was the second breed: Russell terrier. What? The little dog from the show *Frasier*? Yes, Moose was short, but he was stocky; his muscularity was the envy of bodybuilders.

I researched the Russell terrier breed via various websites and found answers that explained many of Moose's behaviors. Russell terriers were bred to hunt foxes. They were trained to run well ahead of their handlers, find a fox, and flush it out. Because Russell terriers are independent hunters, they stop listening to commands and go about their job. When I read that, a realization went off in my head like stadium lights being lit in the middle of the night. It was no wonder Moose wouldn't be recalled once he set his sights on a dog on the other side of the fence.

Russell terriers can also have obstinate temperaments. When this temperament is combined with a hard bite, they can be quite the handful. They typically won't back down from a fight, regardless of the size of their adversary. This reminded me of Moose's infuriation with my trainer's shepherd. Moose was probably a third the size of that dog, but he didn't seem to notice.

Moose was also a fantastic mole hunter. He would often be found bottom up in the air, head in a hole he dug in search of an elusive mole. He spent many hours chasing moles and digging with murderous intent. Many friends have asked to borrow Moose to hunt moles in their yards.

Russell terriers are also known to mark every single square inch of their property. The characteristic "wiping of the feet" dogs do after excreting is not a cleansing ritual; it's a marking ritual. It can be hilarious to watch Moose kick up grass stiff-legged, head held high in the air. On the rare occasion I take Moose off the property, he takes great joy in this ritual. He often kicks his feet so many times, he tears up the turf.

Escape artist is a great nickname for a Russell terrier. Early in Moose's life with me, he taught me how smart he was. I was changing the sheets on my bed while my dogs were in the yard, playing. I looked out the bedroom door and saw I needed to call one of my dogs. I placed my hand on the lever handle on the French door and turned it downward. Suddenly, what was going on outside was no longer an issue. I felt someone was watching me, and the hairs raised on the back of my neck. I turned to look behind me, wondering if someone had really come into my house.

And there he was. Moose had sneaked up behind me and was watching me, tilting his head as I turned the doorknob. Relieved I wasn't living in a horror movie in broad daylight, I laughed and sent Moose on his way.

Moose had the last laugh when I later realized I had taught him how to open lever doors. He would get up on his back feet, put one paw on the doorframe, and used the other to work the lever downward as he pulled the door toward him. This wasn't his only escape skill. I once watched him try to get over the six-foot fence by jumping almost six feet up before he lost traction and came back down the fence.

During the day, my dogs were kept in a four-stall, covered outdoor kennel that resembles a horse barn. Each stall within the kennel has access to a fenced outdoor area. Entrance to the kennel is through a covered hallway. The doors to the runs are secured with simple thumb latches.

It didn't take Moose long to learn to hit the back side of the door hard enough to bounce the latch open. Opening the door leading to the covered area was no problem, because he already knew how to open a latch-handled door. Sometimes I would come home to a happy, free Moose.

He had another skill I didn't train into him: he was able to communicate his desire for a treat to me. My kitchen island is the hub of most of my activity. I plant groceries on the island before putting them away as well as any packages before opening them. I found a great online store that sells made-in-the-US treats at a reasonable price. I would buy a large box of treats that only lasted a month with my five large dogs. Bully sticks, pig's ears, and other assorted goodies give off a powerful smell, even when wrapped in plastic and in a cardboard box.

Moose would sit next to the counter, his ears dropped down. As soon as he caught my eye, his tail would start swooshing the floor. I had no idea at first what he was trying to tell me. I asked him what he wanted. He glanced at the unopened box then glanced back at me. I was amused but not convinced I was being given a message. I would say, "Show me," a few times, and each time he would glance at the box again. Moose learned this was a good way to train me to retrieve what he needed.

As is the case with intelligent human beings, intelligent dogs tend to bore easily. My job was to find an outlet for Moose, find something to keep him both entertained and exhausted. It also needed to be something to bring him joy and calm him at the same time, much like Moose was doing for me.

My other dogs' bloodlines were not as clean. The shelter thought Panzer was a shepherd and Rottweiler mix. It turned out he was neither. One side of his lineage was corgi and Staffordshire terrier mixed with other breeds. The other side was Labrador mixed with other breeds. Of the mixed breeds, the predominant ones were Irish water spaniel and Chinook. It's no wonder Panzer loved to swim, with two water dogs in his background. His shepherd look was from the Chinook. These dogs are close in appearance to the shepherd but lack the black color that is often mixed in.

Ruby's original owner thought she was a border collie mix. I was closer in my assumption of her breed: springer spaniel. One side of her heritage was springer spaniel and the other was malamute. This made sense to me, because Ruby was all about the hair. The ideal temperature for her to be comfortable was thirty degrees and below. I kept her hair super short in the summer, but I hesitated to shave her in the winter. She was miserable inside the house, panting all the time. The other side of Ruby's parenting was clumber spaniel mixed with a few other breeds. The leading breed on that side was an American hairless. I got a good chuckle out of that one.

The shelter believed Cowboy was a mastiff. He did have a large head, but that was due in part to one side of his lineage being Chinese shar-pei. That side had golden retriever mixed with Weimaraner and other breeds. There was a tiny percentage of bull mastiff in there, but his head size was definitely from the shar-pei. The other side of his heritage was American Staffordshire terrier mixed with boxer. Cowboy had the barrel chest of a boxer. His coat was short and stiff, not long and soft like a golden's.

The most surprising to me was Lenny's heritage. Lenny was a long-legged giant breed of dog. I was convinced he had Dane in him. The test said he was half German shorthair pointer. That I could see. What I thought were Dane harlequin markings were the spots of a shorthair. Lenny had the long, floppy ears, spotted chest and feet, and muzzle and tail of his parentage. His other half was so mixed, but the front-runner on that side was Norwegian Buhund. If you aren't familiar with that breed, they are short dogs. Where he got his height from will always be a mystery.

It was fun learning the different breeds in my mixed pack of mutts. Test results also gave me insight into some of their behaviors and preferences. It was striking to me how wrong shelter staff were in assessing breed. It's horrifying how many dogs are killed in shelters because someone considers himself or herself a breed expert. This was the primary reason I wanted to test Moose's DNA. If knowledge is power, I was going to have facts backing me up.

CHAPTER 14

A Champion Is Born

Moose and I had been playing ball for a while. He loved to chase a ball, but it wasn't something I enjoyed much. I tried agility training, but Moose bored of it as fast as I bored of throwing a ball. I changed things up by throwing the ball straight up in the air for him, which he loved. He could jump straight up in the air, twist his body around, and land on his feet. This was a good challenge for his athletic body, and he could perform amazing acrobatics. It was fun and taxing for him.

I watched dog sports competitions on television, hoping for some inspiration. There were a couple of events I thought Moose would be good at. The dock diving event looked like so much fun for the dogs. Moose didn't mind water, but I wasn't sure he would be willing to dive into the water, even for a beloved toy. Whenever I took him to the river, he would allow the cool water to touch his belly, but only for a few minutes. He wouldn't immerse himself.

For me, the show-stopping event was the disc competition. Medium and small dogs dominate disc competitions. They are agile, flexible, fast—and I swear they have wings. Just as talented are their handlers, who are well versed in tossing a disc. Because of Moose's love for jumping in the air and his thick muscular legs, I decided to give it a try.

I hadn't thrown a disc in a good thirty years. I did my research by watching videos on how to throw a disc. Trick throws are not easy to learn, and I don't have any talent in that area, but I tried. I also researched the best discs and found some that not only were made for dogs but were also durable enough to be caught by teeth. There's a big difference between cheap discs and good discs made just for disc competitions. I had my training down and good discs in hand. It was now time to train Moose.

I did some research on how to train dogs to catch a disc. I found a phone app that showed this training step by step. Moose picked it up fast. Part of the initial training was teaching him to track the disc by holding it out and walking in a circle. The human turns in a full circle then throws the disc at the completion. Moose didn't understand what I was trying to teach him with this exercise, because he had always been an attentive student. As I turned in a circle, he would grab the disc before we could complete the circle. I would say no, and he would look at me with that head tilt, wondering what my problem was this time. It was time to call my trainer again.

When Tommy arrived, he asked me what I was trying to do and what the problem was, then asked me to show him. I did, and Moose latched onto the disc. Tommy then did something I find irritating: he fixed it, almost right away. He thought for a few seconds then said, "Okay, give me the disc." He had Moose following him in a circle after two quick attempts. Was I that dumb, or was that guy just a genius? A little bit of both perhaps, although I'm sure he is a genius when it comes to dogs.

He explained that Moose thought I wasn't going to release the disc. Instead, Tommy walked a few feet in the circle and gave the disc to Moose. He got the disc back and did this over and over again while completing the circle. On the second time around, he completed the entire circle, and Moose was off in flight again.

We were now fully armed, Moose and I. I could throw in a straight line, and he could perform like a circus acrobat.

Throwing a disc is as repetitive as throwing a ball, but watching Moose chase down a disc was pure joy for me. The neighbors could hear me whooping and cheering for Moose each time he made an artistic catch. I was having as much fun as Moose, if not more. He was already in incredible shape, but the sprinting and jumping required some conditioning. I could tell when he was getting winded, because his teeth would chatter before he dropped the disc. If he was done chasing the disc but not ready to go inside, he would just run off with the disc. At last I'd found an outlet for the immense energy contained in this medium-size muscle-bound dog.

Moose loved chasing the disc so much he leaped and barked as soon as I get home. My first order of the evening was to play with him. Sometimes we played several times a day. If Moose wanted me to get up and play with him, he had a direct way of communicating this to me. Often I'd find him sitting next to the cabinet where the discs were placed. If he had been sitting silently for a while and I didn't catch on, he would emit a low whimper. I knew what he wanted, but I asked him anyway. He looked at me, then he looked up at the discs. If I felt like teasing him, I'd ask him again. He would telegraph his intent again and again until I grabbed the discs.

If Lenny had energy, he would come outside when I threw the disc for Moose. He would chase Moose with his long-legged gallop, cutting in front of him and enticing him to play. Lenny never tried to take the disc from Moose; he just enjoyed chasing and teasing him. Moose never lost his patience with Lenny, although he dodged all Lenny's efforts to block him. Lenny would tire of chasing Moose pretty quickly and would turn his attention to Ruby. He would follow Ruby around the yard, sniffing her behind. She knew he was there, but she never paid any attention to him.

In all this training, Moose became leaner, more conditioned, and, dare I say, better looking. He went from a scrawny, mangy pup to a muscle-bound dog. His training regimen was as intense and varied as any hard-core athlete.

If I had the drive Moose had, I would use him as my own free personal trainer. On any given day, Moose did a variety of sprints. Some were ridiculously long; some were short and ended in hopping up and down to get a better look at his prey. Moose sprinted whenever he saw a car drive down the road in front of the house and even on the private road on the side of the property. When a vehicle drove by, he would bark at it, "encouraging" it, and then race it to the end of the fence line.

One summer, a carload of young people coming from the river were driving slowly up the road. Moose waited for them at the corner of the fence and barked at them. The passenger laughed and commented to the driver that Moose seemed like he wanted to race. They tested their theory by lurching forward a few feet. Moose began to run then issued more commands to move. Laughter rolled from the car, and then they were off. Moose sprinted down the fence line, keeping up with the car as I yelled my encouragement. The passengers waved to me as they drove off. Those kinds of sprints gave Moose a well-rounded rump and defined, curvaceous thighs.

I've never taken Moose on a distance run. There was nowhere safe to take him, and I didn't think he could focus enough on the run to avoid all the enticements along the way. He got his cardio by digging for moles for hours on end. I would often find him panting next to a hole with dirt covering his tongue and snout. I couldn't get him out of a hole, even if I tried to drag him out of it. Summertime was easy on me, because Moose found so many ways to burn off his endless energy.

Burning so much energy requires long naps. Almost every time a dog gets up after a long nap or sleep, it performs a couple of stretches. These stretches have been copied by yoga enthusiasts and named after their muse. The downward facing dog is a great stretch for the gluteus and hamstrings. The upward facing dog is a fantastic stretch for the chest and abs. Once in a while, after a nice up-dog stretch, Moose will extend his legs backward in a full flex, one after the other.

Panzer became a champion in his own way as well; I didn't

give up on training him. Tommy suggested we teach him nose work. Panzer wasn't toy driven; he was food driven. We used a scented object, and the reward for finding it was a small piece of sausage. At first Panzer didn't understand the nature of the game. Once he picked up on it, he was a superstar. I would place the scented object far out in the field while Panzer was inside the house. I would bring him out, and he would soon find the object. He was amazing and enjoyed the game in small doses. He was also starting to calm down and find comfort in his place in the pack.

Moose was a champion of the hunt as well. I love all animals —even wild ones—and I understand there are some things we can't change about the animal kingdom. I know the facts of life, but I don't have to like that animals have to kill each other to survive.

One week in early 2015, the Pacific Northwest had a stretch of beautiful spring weather. The sun was shining, the birds were nesting, and the dogs were being dogs. They too were enjoying spring's bounty of sights, sounds, and baby critters. It was time for me to feed the dogs before I fed myself. I was unaware an incident would soon set off a comedy of errors on my part. My dogs were going to teach me some important lessons.

I fed Lenny, Panzer, and Ruby and had them shut in their individual rooms. I prepared meals for Cowboy and Moose, but they were still frolicking outside. I was going to have to go get them.

I stepped outside and left the front door open. This was mistake number one. I called the pair and soon spotted them on the grass in front of a tree line. I walked toward them, since they were ignoring my calls. I soon realized the reason I was being ignored. Moose had a small, lifeless rabbit in his mouth. My heart sank.

At this point, I should have just walked away. But I didn't. My dogs did though. Moose picked up the rabbit and started to trot toward the house. He was proud, and he wanted to share the moment with his friends. It was then I realized my mistake in leaving the front door open.

Panic was moving in as fast as Moose picked up his pace. Then I made another mistake. I chased him. And then another mistake: "Don't go in that house!" I yelled, running after him as if he could understand what I was saying. This must have seemed to be an extension of the game to Moose. Now a crazy, screaming, feeble, two-legged runner was chasing the hunter. What fun that must have been for Moose. The thrill of the hunt was over, and it was time to play the keep-away game. He made it all the way into the house. He was guarding his catch, panting from exertion. He was proud of himself, and I had to deal with it. Dogs will be dogs, and I am a fool who maybe learned a lesson or two.

Moose and I trusted each other more at that point, and the pack was finally gelling. We had come to a milestone with recall as well. While the other dogs ran to the fence when another dog was loose, Moose would come back to me when I called him and moved toward him. It wasn't an instant recall; Moose would let the dog know he was there. When he realized he couldn't escape the fence, he would run toward me at breakneck speed. I feared he would knock me over, but there was a loophole in the recall. Moose charged at me then dove off to the side in a move that would be the envy of any football player. He wouldn't let me catch him, not yet. There was time for another pass at the offending dog, then back to me on a recall. He would let me catch him, and he would sit at my feet, staring down the dog while the others barked at the fence line.

Many days I would find Moose lying on the floor, staring out the dog door. He would quietly sit and just watch the world unfolding in front of him. I found myself wondering what he was seeing. Dog vision is so much better than human.

I enjoy watching birds, as did Moose. My intent was to enjoy their beauty and song, while Moose's was to chase and hunt them. If a car drove by or someone walked by on the street, he was out the dog door like a rocket. Other times he would lie on the front porch right outside the front door, holding vigil. He rarely left my sight for long, and he checked in on me almost as much as I checked in on him. We made sure we knew what the other was doing at almost all times.

Progress, we were making progress. I was so glad I chose not to give up on Moose. He made me more confident and calmed me down in the process. Suddenly, life's offenses didn't matter. Any dog lover can profess to the calming abilities of petting one's dog. Moose was always by my side, mirrored my every move from room to room, rode with me in the truck, and slept touching me every night. I felt blessed. Most of all, for the first time in my life I felt unconditionally loved.

Although we as a pack were working things out for the best, I was taking hits in my personal life. On October 16, 2011, the phone rang late at night. Even in my job as a detective subject to call-outs, my heart never gets used to middle-of-the-night phone calls. I woke with a start. It was my father on the other end of the line. All he managed to get out was "We lost your brother." Nothing made sense to my brain. I asked what he meant that my brother was lost. He choked back sobs as he told me my brother was dead. I had known my brother would die young. The last time I saw him, his weight was up to five hundred pounds. He had steadily gained weight after high school and didn't seem to want to get healthy. Now he was gone, and I had to make plans to get back to Texas to pick up the pieces for my parents.

Leaving five dogs to go anywhere is a hassle. Going on a trip longer than a day requires extensive planning. Richard was working odd hours and refused to help with the dogs while I was gone. I recruited my sister-in-law to spend the evenings with them, feed them, and sleep in my room with them. Richard was sleeping in another room by his own choosing. Off to Texas I went. My sister-in-law was a fantastic dog sitter and a relief to my worried mind. Problems within the pack were beginning to pale in comparison to those in my personal life.

CHAPTER 15

The Glue

It took almost six years to have a harmonious home with five dogs. Moose is ever vigilant and remains the best hunter and athlete in the pack. What often gets ignored in dogs like Moose, the high-maintenance dog, is their heart. Moose managed to pull us all through difficult times with his unique leadership skills.

I managed businesses both large and small for ten successful before changing careers. Most good leaders know there's a difference between managing and leading. I was a very efficient manager, and I managed my pack well. But I lacked leadership with the pack. The pack was a complicated mess under my direction. I was lacking the expertise to bring the pack together into a harmonious group. Moose managed to teach me a few things about leadership.

I learned not to manage by fear. Fear causes mistrust, anxiety, and avoidance. Managing by fear can obtain compliance, but it also reduces productivity and the quality of work. Working in fear causes subordinates to seek different leadership or even to plan a coup against the leader.

Be tolerant but know when to issue a correction. Subordinates have their individual quirks as well as their unique gifts. They test boundaries, thereby testing the leader's ability to lead. A leader should be patient but issue a swift and reasonable correction when a line is crossed.

Be confident and fearless. Regardless of the task or the size of the opponent, be ready for the challenge. Leaders must demonstrate the confidence their followers have placed in them. There is no obstacle Moose isn't willing to try to leap, despite his short, stocky frame. The pack senses his confidence and willingly follows him.

Be the first into battle. The challenger must first lay eyes on a leader full of confidence and ability. Moose always leads the charge. He's the first to leap after the bird, dig for the mole, or the chase off the offending dog on the other side of the fence. Once the call for action has been issued, the rest will follow.

Hone your skills. A leader has the skills the followers lack or have not yet fully developed. These skills are essential to survival and thriving, regardless of the mission or task at hand. Moose spends countless hours digging for moles. Sometimes he's successful. Most times he isn't. He chases cars on his side of the fence and develops his speed. He leaps after discs with style and flair, building his leg strength.

Be passionate about your job. Love your job, and the skills will follow. No one willingly follows someone who is just going through the motions. Moose loves to just be a dog. It is his job to lie in the sun, make me laugh, hunt for vermin, and to keep us safe. His passion for his job makes him a natural leader the others are happy to have.

Moose has been a calm, steady influence on the pack and me. He has been a constant companion and playmate for Cowboy. He has taught him courage and confidence in the pack by wrestling with him and often letting him have the upper hand. Lenny learned to make dog friends and most importantly, just how to be a dog again.

I've noticed many changes in myself as well. I now find joy in the simple things. Difficult situations don't stress me as much as they used to. I'm more of a homebody as well. I'm gone long hours during the week, so I try to make up for it on the weekends. My weekends typically look the same. The day starts with a steaming hot cup of coffee touched with real half-and-half. There's nothing better than waking up to a warm cup of brew. As my mind comes around, I check media to see what I missed while I slept. Once I'm informed, I can start my day.

Sundays are not a day of rest for me. They're a day of planning and preparation. Regardless of what I think, Moose always has different plans for my day. He'll let me get away with some cooking, some cleaning, and some yard work. But if I dare to get on the computer, he lets me know how bored he is. A simple sigh lets me know I'm dropping the ball in my duties. I need to get up and throw a ball or a disc many times a day so Moose can get much-needed exercise. Always being a lover of the outdoors, I now have an excuse to go outside every day. Sprints and jumping are on Moose's agenda. A muscle-bound dog needs lots of playtime. When we're done, I can carry on with my chores. But I will be reminded in a few hours that it's time to toss a disc again.

My favorite part of the day is retiring with a good book, another warm drink in hand, and Moose by my side. If I'm staying up too late, Moose will stand in the hallway that leads to my bedroom, let out a soft whimper, and stare at me. I can't just put him in bed; I have to join him. I sit on the bed, working on the computer, reading, or watching TV, while Moose contently snoozes, touching some part of my body. The rest of the dogs quickly join us on their selected beds.

Moose is not a thoughtful sleeping companion. His comfort is of the utmost importance. One thing is certain: he has to be touching me most of the night. So many times I've woken with a backache because of the awkward positions I was forced to sleep in. If my sciatica is acting up, finding comfort is pure torture. These are the things dog lovers sacrifice for the love of our dogs. The most endearing sleeping position that I have awoken to is Moose stretched out back to back with me. When he realizes that I'm waking, he scoots his head up to be even with my head.

Most of the time I am healthy. I rarely succumb to the flu or to colds. What I dread most is the stomach flu. One fall day, my luck had run out. I became sick with a flu determined to clean out every inch of my digestive system. I was miserable—up and down, up and down for hours, trying to get rid of the bug in my system. I had been that sick one other time in my past. I was nineteen years old, and I tore my esophagus heaving. By the time I got to the hospital, I was near death with the bleeding and the dehydration. That episode was in the back of my mind with this flu. I tried to drink some Sprite to settle my stomach and to get some fluids in me.

While I was going back and forth between my bed and the bathroom, Moose followed me. He would jump off the bed when I went to the bathroom and sit on the floor in front of me, waiting for my bout to be over. He would then jump back on the bed with me. Moose had a rigorous leg workout that day.

On my final purging trip to the bathroom, Moose followed me in like the true friend he was. He sat in front of me sideways, facing the door. He was still. He looked forward and waited for me to regain some sort of dignity. He reminded me of a soldier standing guard, silent, noble, and brave. In his way he was providing me with the support he felt I needed. I was honored to have him stand guard at my side. This is not appealing, but as I sat on the toilet, my stomach decided to get rid of the Sprite I'd drunk earlier. I spewed Sprite onto Moose's head. I felt even more horrible when he closed his eyes but maintained his position like the great morale soldier he was. I cleaned him up, and he happily jumped back in bed with me. My love and respect deepened for him that night.

I decided I needed to go to the hospital to stop my fluid loss. I didn't want another repeat of that day many years ago. Richard drove me to the emergency room with Moose by my side. Moose waited in the truck for me while the hospital stabilized me. With medication on board, I was no longer ridding my body of fluids. Back at home, I slept soundly for hours with my nursemaid by my side. I couldn't have asked for a better friend. Moose wasn't prone to illnesses, so it was hard for me to return the favor. I was indebted to him for showing me he would stand by me however long it took me to regain my strength. Moose was a true friend indeed.

It turned out I wasn't the only one Moose looked out for. Late one night, I heard Cowboy licking incessantly. I knew from research that dogs lick when they are feeling nauseated. I jumped out of bed, as did Moose and Cowboy. We quickly made it to the front door, where Cowboy made a mad dash for the yard with Moose close behind. The first time this happened, I went to check on Cowboy and found him eating grass but not quite ready to come in. Moose was close by, inspecting the creatures of the night he'd located in the grass. When Cowboy was ready to come in, Moose was right behind him.

More than anything, Moose brought joy into my life. Whether it be an expression, an antic, or one of his many quirks, rarely a day went by that Moose didn't manage to make me smile. Moose is a treasured gift to me. I wanted to share him with the world and lift other people's spirits as well. Since Moose wasn't tolerant of other dogs and couldn't be a therapy dog, I found another way to share his joy with the world. I created a Facebook page for him and simply called Moose's Page. I posted almost daily and achieved the desired effect. Moose's handsome mug was making people fall in love with him, and his silly expressions and antics made people smile.

Once again, it was time for my personal life to take a hit. One bright, beautiful September day in 2012, Richard decided to move out. My thoughts were how to protect my dogs and keep them safe and in my house. By January I was divorced. I had moments when I considered rehoming some of my dogs. Running a house on acreage with five dogs while working full time seemed an insurmountable task. My thoughts turned to finances and having to work overtime to make ends meet. My dogs deserved better than having to be kenneled all the time.

Love is a powerful motivator. I enlisted in Angela's help. She would help me by letting my dogs out during the day for potty breaks. She didn't want me to move any more than I wanted to move. I could have purchased a cheaper, easier-to-care-for house, but I would have to fully fence a yard again. Renting was out of the question. I had to find a way to make living in the house work for us.

CHAPTER 16

Moving On

It is hard to keep a secret at work, especially when you work with people you consider your family. Then there are those who pop into your office and say, "Hey, what's new with you?" My friend Cole, the one I had lunch with after Snickers died, was one of those that asked me that question. I told him what had happened. Cole listened, offered his sympathy, then told me, "Well, you just keep moving forward. It's all you can do." I let that soak in. Once again, Cole had offered the perfect consolation. I needed to just move forward.

After living by ourselves for several months, I ended up making an incredible sacrifice. I let Richard move back in. He was to be a roommate and nothing more. I needed help managing the property and the dogs; Richard knew how to do both. He rented a room from me on the opposite end of the house.

We got along well for the most part, because I didn't care about the things that married couples fight about. It was awkward, embarrassing, and impossible to explain to people why I lived with my ex. Those closest to me couldn't understand how I could stand to be around him. What was important to me was making sure my dogs had a safe place where they would be taken care of. It isn't about me when innocent lives are depending on me. Their love for me was unconditional. I was learning to give that back. They wouldn't thrive under anyone else's care.

Things were going well at the house. The dogs were getting along, bills were getting paid, and I was plugging away. I had become incredibly diligent in managing the dogs' personalities. I rarely if ever let Panzer out alone with any of the dogs except Ruby. If Moose was outside, I monitored his activities, making sure he wasn't charging the fence at dogs walking by.

One late spring afternoon, I came home from work, played with the dogs, then went inside to change for my workout. It took me maybe two minutes to change into my workout clothes. I looked around me and saw only three dogs. Moose and Panzer were no longer in the house.

I went outside and called the boys. Moose and Panzer started walking toward me from a patch in the grass where there were a few mole holes. As they walked, they looked at each other. I knew this wasn't a good sign, and I urged them to hurry up. They stopped looking at each other and focused on me, coming at a quick trot. When Moose reached me, I could see his neck was wet. Upon further inspection, I saw a hole in his neck and blood on the inside of his ear. I inspected Panzer and saw the whole nape of his neck was wet.

It was obvious to me Moose had been digging in a hole, and Panzer had grabbed him and pulled him out. They must have fought and ended it when I came out, calling for them. I was upset Panzer had done damage to Moose, irritated at myself for dropping my guard, and relieved it wasn't worse.

The following day I took Moose to the vet. The damage to Moose's ear would heal quickly. Panzer didn't have any visible injuries. After this incident, relations between the dogs calmed quite a bit. Panzer would still try to bully Moose while he dug for a mole. I was always on top of watching the two of them and correcting Panzer immediately. I don't know if they came to some understanding that day, but I hoped with my diligence they wouldn't fight again. The pack was calming down, but my personal life was about to be turned upside down again.

The loss of my brother was devastating to my father. My brother had never left home, and he and my father had formed a tight bond. I was the black sheep for leaving home. The last time my brother spoke to me, he had called me and berated me for leaving the state. He called me names and considered me to be demon spawn. I told him I forgave him, and I hung up the phone. I had left him in stunned silence. My father had taken a spill, and my brother was tired of having to take care of aging parents. He wasn't the kind to seek outside help for anything, hence his incredible weight gain. Instead, he did what he knew how: he lashed out at me.

That fall was the beginning of my father's decline. After my brother's death, he hired someone to drive him around and to help take care of matters around the house. I had offered my home to my parents, but they both refused, each blaming the other for not wanting to move. My father had been in and out of the hospital many times in his later years. Throughout his life, he had suffered from major medical issues but always bounced back from them. In his late seventies, this was no longer the case.

On December 21, 2013, I received a phone call from my mother. She said my father was in the hospital again. She couldn't explain to me the nature or urgency of his condition. I asked if I needed to go down there, and she told me he would be fine and I didn't need to come. I spoke to my father's hired help. He told me my father had an infection, and the doctors and nurses were vague about his prognosis. My father was unable to speak coherently to me, so I spoke to a nurse. She told me she couldn't tell me much due to privacy laws, but she felt I should come to see my father.

I contacted an attorney and had him meet my parents at the hospital and draw up power of attorney papers and a will for my father. I didn't know if my father had such documents, and I knew my mother wouldn't know. There were many tasks I needed to complete so I could fly out on short notice. Work was accommodating. The airlines were another story. I paid handsomely to be able to fly out on December 24. Arrangements were made for the dogs, and this time Richard helped out quite a bit.

On December 23, I wrapped up final arrangements and took Cowboy to the vet for his annual checkup. While I was at the vet, my cousin called my cell phone several times. When I finally was able to call her back, she told me my father had passed that afternoon. I flew back home and helped my mother handle the overwhelming task of handling their estate.

My mother was incredibly helpless. She asked me if my father should be cremated or buried. I told her it wasn't my decision to make. She said they had never discussed such matters. My mother flat-out refused to make the decision about my father's remains. She insisted I do it.

I searched my father's office, hoping for clues. Sitting next to his computer was a packet issued by the US Army. It was an end-of-life informational packet for the veteran to fill out. My father had completed it and left it where it could be found. I wondered if he knew he wasn't coming back this time. He wanted to be cremated. I was glad, because that's the decision I would have been forced to make for him.

I did what I could for my mother. There is so much to be done when someone passes. When I got back home, Richard picked me up, and Moose was in the front seat, welcoming me home.

A week later, Harleigh Ann, my cat that was living with Angela, succumbed to cancer. Once again I had to make the end-of-life decision. Angela refused to decide when she should go, but I refused to let her suffer. A sweet soul, she lived to be just shy of twenty years old.

The following March, the earth moved several miles to the east of my home. A massive landslide measuring one square mile killed forty-three people. This hit so close to home. Fears of further catastrophic damage in the form of flash flooding caused a mandatory evacuation. I had learned from the floods to be prepared with emergency kits for humans and dogs. The kits were packed into my truck, and all five dogs were loaded into Richard's truck and mine.

All the hotels I called were full. I had friends offer to let us stay in their homes. But they were also dog owners. My dogs were used to sleeping with me. There was no way I could throw them in a stranger's backyard and expect them to be comfortable and feel secure. I declined the offers.

We spent the night at a rest stop. Panzer and Ruby slept in the cab of Richard's truck. Lenny, Cowboy, and Richard slept in the bed of my truck, which was covered with a canopy. Moose slept in my front seat, and I slept in my back seat. It was miserable and cold, but we were safe and together. The following morning we were allowed to return home. We were spared any catastrophic events.

The crisis was over on the personal side. At work, there was a lot to be done. An unbelievable amount of debris had to be cleaned up. The scope of the slide was hard to fathom. I remember going to the site and being amazed by the quiet and the mountain of dirt where there used to be a highway. The thousands of volunteers sitting under tents eating a meal humbled me. The canine handlers slept on the ground with their dogs. I wasn't skilled in search and rescue or in any kind of recovery. My job was to make death notifications and provide security for the presidential visit.

Seven months later, an event occurred that caused me to have serious doubt about my choice in careers. A man went on a shooting rampage and shot up two police stations and an unoccupied police vehicle. In his path of destruction, his next stop was another police station. On his way, he encountered several police officers. He fired several shot at them, hitting one of them. How none of them had serious injuries is beyond me.

One week later, a boy developed a malicious plan. He took a handgun from his home, asked friends to join him for lunch, then proceeded to take head shots at those children. He made sure they wouldn't survive the attack. When an adult intervened, he turned the gun on himself and took another fatal shot.

While I was trying to manage emergencies, I had to deal with my mother's declining mental health. She went from a woman with purpose to a depressed woman who wanted nothing more than to join her son and husband in the afterlife. The stress of managing two lives, one long-distance, was unbelievable, and it was taking its toll. I did what I could, but I wasn't going to move back home.

I will never win an award for daughter of the year, and I'm okay with that. I'm a contributing member of society. I'm educated, and I work in public service. I rescue dogs, I recycle, and I help people every chance I get. And yet people judged me. Some do a poor job of trying to veil their contempt. Others just come out and tell me I was a terrible daughter. I used to let it bother me, but I don't anymore.

My parents were not affectionate people. There were never any hugs, no long talks, no doing anything together, and no I-love-yous. We coexisted, and I was told to figure out life's mysteries on my own. I did. I got an education, worked to gain some skills, and then moved two thousand miles away from home. It wasn't easy, but I made it. In time, I managed to make a pretty good life for myself.

I hired home health care workers to stay with my mother. Her in-home care was peppered with visits to the hospital. She refused to move in with me or with any other family member. She also refused to move into an assisted living facility. The pressure of trying to manage her life as well as mine was eating at me. I wasn't sure how much more I could take. The one constant in my life was my dogs. Every time I came home, I was greeted with joy and love. They were my stress relief.

Then the day came that changed everything for my mother. She fell once again. Her health care workers said she was in a lot of pain, so they took her to the hospital. There she stayed for a few days. She was then sent to a rehabilitation facility. It quickly became clear she had dementia. I decided I needed to educate myself on the disease, since no one involved in her care was helping me understand it. I learned that dementia is horrible for both the victims and their families.

I never knew what I was going to get when I spoke to my mother. Many times she didn't know who I was. A few times she thought I was her cousin and spoke to me only in Armenian, her native language. It was hard to take, but I played along. I had lost my mother for the first time. I would lose her again at her death.

What I learned from those conversations was that my mother had forgotten my brother's death three years before. She also forgot that my father had died over a year before. She told "her cousin" that neither my brother nor I had been to visit. I saw no sense in opening old wounds, so I offered the excuse "Maybe they're busy." She said we weren't; we were just away at school and didn't have anyone to bring us to see her. I found it was better for the both of us to lie to her.

My mother stayed in the facility for over one hundred days. When it came time to move her, I was blessed to find a loving caregiver, which changed everything for me and for my mother. The changes for me were positive. Having reliable care for my mother reduced my stress levels quite a bit. Mother gained weight and stopped falling. She stopped complaining about her care, and her health made a vast turn-around. The horrific part for her was being removed from her house, never to return. That broke my heart.

Yes, police officers have to be tough and resilient, but at our core we are human. These things do affect us and sometimes cause irreparable damage. Having to deal with so much death and loss caused me to develop phobias about my own mortality. I feared flying because the plane might crash. Driving scared me because someone might come head-on into my lane. My job scared me because we were easy targets.

Often I found myself worrying about what would happen to my dogs if I died suddenly. Five dogs with special needs is a lot for anyone to handle. Dogs such as mine often suffer in shelters and are put down. I worried the most about Moose. Dog-aggressive dogs are often quickly put down in shelters instead of being given a chance.

It became hard for me to walk out the door when I had to leave for work. Like most adults, I was being pulled in a million different directions. I had to go to work. We needed food, shelter, and basic comforts. Work needed me. There were so many things that needed to be done. Work always insisted I give it more and more of my time.

I am a fixer of things. I am the one that rights the wrongs for many people. I do what is asked of me, and I give all I have—my mind, my time, and my presence. I love what I do, but I love my life more.

I worried about what happened while I was away from home. I worried about the loneliness, the solitude, and the inevitable happening while I am gone. As much as I dread the moment when my dogs will leave my life, I want to be the one who is with them when they go. I want to hold them and comfort them, whispering my adorations into their ear as they cross to the other side.

On my way home, my thoughts weren't filled with the tasks I left undone or the ones I didn't have a chance to get to. No, those tasks would still be there tomorrow. They would be there for the person who takes my place when I finally leave my job. There would never be a day when there's no work to do.

My thoughts are on the unconditional love I receive when I walk in the door. For my dogs, their long-lost friend has returned. They greet me with joyful barking, running around in circles, and jumping for joy. No person can make anyone feel that special. We spend time together outside, regardless of the weather. We play, we enjoy each other's company, and then it's time again to get ready for the next day. I just hope that it's enough and that their hearts are filled with the love I try to return.

I sought help in dealing with my phobias, and I prayed. I realized my phobias were based on what I couldn't control. I focused instead on what I could control. I made plans for my dogs' care in case I passed. I also made sure I gave my dogs a life they would enjoy to its fullest.

Panzer and Ruby were passionate swimmers, so I bought a large bone-shaped pool. I built a frame for it like a deck and placed it next to their kennels. In the summer, it's always full and a relief for the dogs on a sweltering day. I also had a dog shower built in my laundry room. This one was more for my convenience, since the dogs didn't care for baths. Panzer and Ruby loved the water and never resisted. Moose didn't mind baths, but he hated the tile base. Cowboy and Lenny were another story. Those two were the most in need of baths. They both had oily coats, and their black fur showed the grease and dirt fast. Any time Cowboy got near standing water, he would only let it come up around his feet. He despised baths, and it was a challenge to get him in the shower. Baths petrified Lenny. Once in the shower, he would shiver until I dried him off. They all recovered fast, as I had a nice treat waiting for them when they were toweled off.

I felt safe at night being surrounded by five dogs. Moose slept on my bed, and the other four slept on beds surrounding my own. Moose was hypervigilant and would often wake me with a start as he burst into a barking fit. Once I could hear again over the noise of my own heartbeat, I would hear the yip, yip, yip call of coyotes. I enjoyed listening to the unique sound of coyotes, but I knew they were baiting my dogs and the neighbors' dogs. I also wished they would sing their song before eleven o'clock at night.

There were other sounds in the night as well. Despite Cowboy having an average-length snout, being part shar-pei caused him to be an avid snorer. Often his snores and chortles would wake me. Most times he snored like a human, but other nights he made the funniest sounds. Like many people living with snorers, the sound was a comforting reminder the snorer was still alive.

Lenny, being an old dog, often needed to go outside in the middle of the night. He also loved cookies, especially as an evening snack. Somehow he managed to turn the nighttime potty break into what I dubbed the cookie game. Like clockwork, at eight o'clock in the evening, Lenny would go to the front door and scratch. I would get up to let him out, and he would stand at the door, staring into the dark night. I would grab his collar and try to nudge him out. He wouldn't budge—his feet planted firm on the ground.

Before I caught on to what Lenny wanted, I would shut the door and go back to bed. He would again scratch at the door. And once again, he wouldn't go out. He would turn around and prance to the cookie jar, staring at me with ears lifted high. Every single time I gave in to him. He would eat his cookie, and we would often repeat the routine again. On the third scratch, Lenny would go outside to potty. He manipulated me, but I didn't mind. He was a sweet old dog that rarely asked for anything besides a tasty treat or two or three. I gave Lenny all the cookies he wanted.

A year after that most tumultuous year, a dear friend of mine, Samuel, asked me if he could get married at my house. I agreed, even though he told me he was going to invite almost three hundred people to the wedding. I didn't think the dogs would be a problem, even though I had never had that many people at my house. The big day was going to be in the summer. It would be a test to see how far my dogs had come.

CHAPTER 17

Saying Good-Bye

One spring morning in early 2015, Lenny came in after his walk in the yard, and I noticed blood on the ground where he had just walked. I found blood coming from a paw pad and assumed he had stepped on something. When the bleeding didn't stop, I made an appointment with his vet. The vet looked at the pad, cleaned it, and sent Lenny back home with specific instructions about keeping the pad clean and dry. A week later, the pad wasn't getting any better.

That same week, I felt a lump in the side of Lenny's face. I assumed it was a fatty deposit; it was perfectly round. I knew this because I had found a few round lumps on Moose's body that were confirmed to be fatty deposits. But Lenny wasn't his usual self. He relinquished many of his meals, which wasn't like him. He also rarely got up off the couch anymore.

Lenny and I went back to the vet to check on his foot. That day I struggled to get him in my truck. At 120 pounds, he wasn't easy to lift. He also stumbled getting in because of his foot.

Lenny had a tendency to "pancake" when he was afraid. He would crouch down, make himself flat, and freeze. It was hard, but I managed to lift his back end and get him into my truck. Once in the office, Lenny was more comfortable, and his easygoing nature took over. I mentioned to the vet the lump in

Lenny's mouth. He pulled back his gums to reveal a nasty tumor that needed to be removed.

We talked about Lenny's foot, and he told me he suspected the foot and the tumor were cancerous. He left it up to me to decide what to do. Lenny was almost fourteen years old, a remarkably long life for a giant breed dog. I told the vet to remove the tumor and the toe that was infected. I left Lenny there that evening, and he would have surgery the following day. I wanted so badly for surgery to be the cure he needed.

I picked Lenny up two days later. With the toe removed, he could function much better. True to his personality, he hadn't wanted to eat at the vet's office. He also was stubborn in his refusal to relieve himself on lead. The vet's wife and I laughed later when she told me how she and her husband tried to keep Lenny corralled in the yard behind the building. The facility isn't fenced, and they used their bodies to keep him there. They decided his recovery would be quicker if Lenny came home.

Loading Lenny into my truck went much easier. He jumped right in the back, proving his resiliency once again. It was as if the past two days had not resulted in the removal of his toe and a large tumor in his mouth.

Within a week, the old Lenny returned. He learned to maneuver without the toe, and his mouth healed fast. The vet was surprised at his rapid recovery. He had said the same thing to me a few short months prior, when Lenny had a bad reaction to an NSAID. They had expected him to die. I hadn't. I knew Lenny wasn't done yet. I wasn't surprised, and I was cautiously optimistic.

One week later we had a follow-up appointment. The test results had come in on the toe and the mouth tumor. Lenny had malignant melanoma. The vet said I could consult with a cancer specialist. I decided at Lenny's age every day was a gift, and I wasn't going to make him suffer car rides and treatments that most likely wouldn't work.

On the ride home, I knew Lenny had cancer, but he didn't know. Just being present is one of the blessings of being a dog.

I glanced toward the back of my truck and saw him sitting up and looking out the side window. With the back bench seat folded, he was tall enough to be able to look out the window. He was enjoying the ride, completely unaware he was living on borrowed time. It brought me peace to see him enjoying his ride, living in the moment. In that moment, without knowing, he changed my perspective.

A few days later, he had one of the best days he'd had in a long time. He was outside when I came home from work. This was a rare occurrence. When he heard my tires on the pavement, he picked up his head, perked up his ears, and came running to greet me at the gate. He followed my truck, galloping behind it. When I got out of the truck, he galloped some more. That night he ate like he did when he was feeling well. It was a great day, and we both knew it. I was so happy. Every day after that was a bit of a struggle, but I ignored the fact he had cancer. We just enjoyed each day for the gift that it was.

I did my own research and found nothing but bad news. Malignant melanoma is a fast-moving cancer that often takes a life in short time. In a matter of a couple of months, my dog had gone from a carefree to not being able to use his back leg and having a giant tumor in his mouth. Many websites mentioned when the cancer was in the mouth and foot, it was already in the later stages. It surprised me these were common locations for melanoma. The websites also said the pet would have mere months, if that long, to live.

A month later I found more lumps in Lenny's neck. I took him back to the vet, who confirmed the cancer was in his lymph nodes. He felt his spleen, and it was enlarged. He said the cancer was most likely there as well. I asked how long he thought Lenny had. He said five months at the most.

Dogs don't fear what the future holds. I decided I wouldn't either. You wouldn't have known Lenny had cancer. He trotted around the yard, chased Moose, followed Ruby around, and maintained a healthy appetite. The nighttime cookie game continued daily.

In the meantime, my mother's dementia was progressing. She had become completely unaware that my father and brother were dead. At this point she too turned a corner. She had been angry about being in a rehab facility. Now that her dementia had progressed, she was just happy. It was clear when I talk to her, and others had noticed the same thing. Maybe there's a peace that comes with just living in the moment, unaware that life has already taken most of what you hold dear.

During the summer of 2015, I had to return to my hometown to sell my mother's belongings as well as the home I grew up in. She had advanced to the point in her decline where she would never be able to take care of herself or live on her own again. I had no choice but to get rid of her belongings, which neither she nor I could take care of. The task was a major undertaking, and I scheduled a week for myself to take care of everything.

It is haunting having to get rid of someone else's memories. The guilt was overwhelming, but I couldn't ask my mother what she wanted to keep. She was lost in a time when my brother and I were children. My father was still alive in her mind as well but always in the hospital.

I managed to pull it off; a deadline is a powerful thing. I sold the house, its contents, and the cars. I also visited my mother almost every day. She knew me at first but then would forget who I was after a few minutes. I was blessed to have the best caretaker I could hope for to take care of her. I left her in capable hands.

An interesting thing happened when I shut the door to my childhood home for the last time. I had lived in that home for eighteen years—from four years old to twenty-two. Those were my formative years. People asked me if I would miss the house. Some asked if it makes me sad to sell it. My response was always a definite no. I hated going home to visit my parents after I moved out. And I finally knew why.

It was that house. I have not a single happy memory of living there. When I walked into the bedroom where I'd spent many years, I remembered shoving furniture against the door.

My brother would have fits of rage, and I was the recipient. If I shut and locked my door, he would take the doorknob off. I would shove furniture against the door and hide in my closet. He always managed to find his way in.

My bedroom was also where my father sent me when he could no longer stand the sight of me. It was my refuge—the place I cried, the place I dreamed of my future life somewhere I was safe, the place I kept my secrets from the world.

The dining room had many memories for me. The wall in the dining room is where my father pinned me and told me to take it like a man. In that same room, my father told me he was going to kill me and then chased me out the front door. The dining room was where my father threw a heavy glass object at me when I placed it the wrong way on the dining-room table. It was also the place where I took my final beating from my father, the day I finally told him it was going to be me or him, and I didn't care which.

When I left the house at twenty-two, I knew I would never live there again. No matter how bad my life got, I knew without a doubt I wouldn't be back. So, no, I wouldn't miss the house or what it represented for me. Shutting the door for the last time was shutting the door on my little house of horrors—the place where I was never safe and no one protected me from evils, the place where mental health issues went ignored and untreated. I am not angry and don't hold grudges. I'm relieved to finally be free to move on and heal. Now when I go back to visit my mother, I can stay in a hotel and maybe enjoy my stay.

For this trip, Richard came home right after work and took care of the dogs. I worried Lenny would take a turn for the worse while I was gone. I didn't want to let him down and not be there for him when he passed. I owed it to him—as I had owed it to Snickers—to be there, stroke his head, and reassure him. It wasn't a task I looked forward to but a duty and an honor I had to fulfill. Lenny did well while I was gone and greeted me with joy when I got home.

Two months later, it was time for the wedding I had agreed to host. Samuel and I had worked hard getting ready for it. We put lots of time into the grounds, always with dogs at our heels. The wedding was on a summer day, but the skies were hazy, not clear and beautiful as is the norm in the Pacific Northwest. Just on the other side of the mountains, a record wildfire was burning acres upon acres of land. The smoke carried over, but it took nothing from the day.

Lenny, Cowboy, Ruby, and Panzer stayed in the house most of the day, going out for the occasional potty break. Moose was a different story. There were people at the house from the early hours, and he wanted to be a part of all the festivities. He enjoyed meeting everyone and made the rounds, if for nothing else but to sniff everyone or brush up against him or her.

Before the ceremony, the wedding party was having some fun. Two of the groomsmen were on the dance floor with a young boy, practicing break dancing. When the boy was on his back and having a hard time getting up, one of the men reached down to help him up. And Moose began his slow stalk. I realized what he was doing and grabbed his leash. He thought the older male was picking on the boy, and he wasn't going to allow it. Up until that point I hadn't seen Moose be protective of a child.

Once the festivities started, I took Moose inside so he wouldn't bother anyone. He sat at the door and whimpered. I relented and took him out on the leash. He was happy just to sit and watch all the people.

About every half hour, we would walk through the crowds, and people would smile and pet Moose as he brushed past. One woman in particular was of special interest to him. She was wearing a knee-length dress with a flowing skirt. Moose kept bumping up her skirt with his muzzle and letting the skirt hang over his eyes. I apologized and said I didn't know why he was doing that. She laughed and said he must like dresses. She had a coworker whose dog did the same thing whenever he saw a woman in a dress.

I was impressed that Moose was so composed with so many people surrounded him. He seemed to be in his element. He enjoyed everyone—young and old, male and female. He even got on the dance floor with the groom and wagged his tail while observing everyone dance. It was one of the most beautiful weddings I've ever been lucky to be a part of. I'm glad Moose shared that special day with me.

We were now five months past Lenny's cancer diagnosis. He was starting to have difficulty getting up off the floor. I didn't think much of it, because old dogs—and especially big old dogs—have a hard time with hard floors. Richard or I would just wrap our arms around his hindquarters and help him get up.

It was a Sunday in September, and the day started off just like any other. The days were long, and the skies were clear. The dogs had eaten and enjoyed a lazy weekend morning. All was well. Around noon, Richard found Lenny lying on the floor. He urged me to come take a look and insisted something wasn't right. I looked at Lenny, and he was stiff. Not wanting to believe the worst, I asked him if he wanted a cookie. He didn't budge. Looking closer, Lenny's eyes seemed to be bulging, and his neck was straight but his limbs were mobile. Richard said he had found him on the floor in a pile of drool. No manner of prompting could get him to move. We tried to move him, but he flailed his legs.

I called the emergency vet and gave a rundown of what I was seeing. They said I should bring him in. Getting a 120-pound, immobile dog loaded in a truck was going to be a challenge. I was afraid to move Lenny and cause him any damage. We managed to get a small rug underneath him, but we couldn't pick him up without causing discomfort. Richard went to find a large board, and I called the neighbor to come help. We managed to load Lenny into the back of the truck, where Richard rode with him. I drove with Moose riding next to me in the front seat.

The drive to the emergency vet took half an hour. That was plenty of time for reality to sink in. I knew this was it. A fourteen-year-old body riddled with cancer was a lot for a dog to handle. I drove staring straight ahead on the country highway, thinking about what this all meant. Moose sat next to me, staring out the window, enjoying the ride. I tried not to cry, because crying meant I'd accepted defeat.

I pulled into the emergency clinic parking lot, went inside, and asked them to bring a gurney to help get Lenny inside. When I turned around to head back outside, I lost it. I knew this was going to be it.

Once inside, it took the vet an hour to come see us. During that time, Richard and I alternated sitting on the floor with Lenny, comforting him and letting him know we were there. I noticed Lenny's eyes were rolling up and down. At one point, he picked up his head and dragged his tongue across the roof of his mouth several times. I took this as a sign he was getting better.

When the vet finally came in, he dashed all hope of a recovery. He said that the cancer had most likely spread to Lenny's brain in the form of a tumor and that the tumor had probably affected his motor function. He further explained the licking was because the involuntary movement of Lenny's eyes, or nystagmus, was causing him to be nauseated. I asked if Lenny would recover from this, and he told me no.

I agreed to let Lenny go. The vet reassured me by saying he would do the same thing for his dog. That helped, but I lost all power of speech as the tears flowed down my cheeks.

I asked if I could bring a dog in to be with Lenny during this time. The vet agreed, and I told him Moose was an animal-aggressive dog. He said it wouldn't be a problem to get him inside, but cautioned that sometimes dogs turn on each other when one of them is dying. I felt confident Moose wouldn't turn on Lenny, so I went to get him.

Moose was eager to get out of the truck and go into this new place he had never been in before. The lobby of the clinic is wide. Once inside the doors, the waiting area is to the left, patient rooms are to the right, and the reception is in the center. At the end of the patient rooms is a swinging door that leads to more waiting rooms. Those doors were where I had to get Moose without incident.

My plan was to run down the hallway to Lenny's room. As we

entered the reception area, I noticed they had all the dogs moved to the far side of the room. I was moving fast, trying to get past the lobby, when I felt resistance that almost pulled the harness off Moose.

The entrance doors had a large carpet in front of them. The rest of the area had tile. In my rush to get Moose in safely, I had forgotten his dread of walking on hard surfaces. But with a little encouragement, he took the tile like a champion. We made it into the room without incident.

Moose came in the room and sniffed Lenny. Lenny picked up his head and sniffed. He lay his head back down, now a bit calmer than before. His old friend had come to see him off. Moose sat calmly with Richard while I lay back down with Lenny.

When the time came for the fatal injection, I was lying on the floor, one arm around Lenny's body, the other stroking his head. I talked to him and reassured him everything was all right. It didn't take long. I knew the exact moment he took his last breath. I put my hand in front of his nose then felt his heart. The vet, seeing what I was doing, confirmed my observation. He left me with my head buried in Lenny's neck, crying and saying good-bye to my old friend. My choice was to cremate him, so Lenny had to stay where he was.

Moose and I exited the building without incident. During the drive home, Moose and Richard shared the front seat while I drove. Moose was going to sit in Richard's lap, then he turned his head and looked at me. I gave him a half-hearted smile. Moose turned around, sat next to me, placed his head on my chest, and closed his eyes. His head stayed on my chest for the rest of the ride home.

A week and a half later, I received a phone call that Lenny's remains were ready for pickup. I can't explain why, but it made me happy. I was going to bring Lenny home. I'm not one to linger on death or to see much value in the rituals of funerals. But this felt right. Maybe someday I will spread Lenny's ashes, but for now his box sits on a table next to a window overlooking the front yard. I decorated his box with his name and lifespan in glitter letters. His collar is wrapped around the box just below that.

The biggest surprise to me was Cowboy's change in behavior after Lenny's death. On the mornings I went to work, I put Panzer, Ruby, and Moose in the kennel. Cowboy never wanted to be locked up in the kennel, so I would let him roam free during the day with Lenny. My two lowest-energy dogs patrolled the grounds for me during the day. Cowboy would alert Angela to any perceived intruders with his loud bark.

After Lenny passed, Cowboy started to follow me and the other dogs out to the kennel and would jump on one of the empty beds. I realized he now wanted to stay in the kennel with his pack, so I put a bed in there for him. Cowboy was happy to sleep at his post until Angela came to give potty breaks and cookies. She left the door open for him in case he wanted to explore. By the afternoon, he was almost always out and about, patrolling the grounds. I had no idea Cowboy would miss Lenny. For me, it shows how much unexpressed love lies in our dogs.

I've been less than perfect in raising my dogs and in being human, but I'm willing to learn. I am lucky to be surrounded by dogs that could care less if I'm perfect. They don't have a concept of what perfection is. That is a human flaw.

My dogs will continue to be the priority in my life. Every day with them is a blessing. I'm fortunate to have my mentors, my guides, my loves, my dogs by my side. Through them I've learned joy in the simple things, patience, and understanding. Moose has shown me I'm worthy of extreme devotion and dedication. He has tried to teach me the most important lesson: to love unconditionally. I'm a slow learner, and I have baggage to discard, but I am ever willing to keep working on myself. Through it all, I have the one thing I need the most: the love of Moose.

Author's Note: The first version of "For The Love Of Moose" published in April of 2016. The following chapters are a continuation of the original story.

First - I want to say 'thank you' to everyone who read my book and gave me feedback. The comment I got the most was, "Thanks for making me cry in the first chapter." You are welcome. I say it with love not sarcasm. You see, we are part of an exclusive club. We are those who love the innocents, who love without question and forgive without judgement. We are those who love dogs the moment we meet them to include the ones we have never met. When we hear a tragic story, it brings us to tears. I cry when people talk about losing their beloved pet. I have fallen in love with dogs upon meeting them or reading about them.

I will tell you this. If you continue to read, I plan to make you cry again. We can't have life without death.

> *"There is a cycle of love and death that shapes the lives of those who choose to travel in the company of animals. It is a cycle unlike any other. To those who have never lived through its turnings and walked its rocky path, our willingness to give our hearts with full knowledge that they will be broken seems incomprehensible. Only we know how small a price we pay for what we receive; our grief, no matter how powerful it may be, is an insufficient measure of the joy we have been given."* — Suzanne Clothier, Bones Would Rain from the Sky: Deepening Our Relationships with Dogs

CHAPTER 18

Growing Older Together

The pack was getting up in age. Ruby was the oldest at at twelve, Panzer was eleven, Cowboy was ten and Moose nine. These ages are impressive for large and extra large dogs. The typical life span of these breeds of dogs are respectively, thirteen, twelve, eight and twelve.

Overall, my dogs were healthy seniors. Ruby had arthritis in her front elbows. Supplements were little relief for her. She would often drop onto her bed at the end of the night. Slowly lowering herself was more painful than collapsing onto her bed.

Panzer had spondylosis which is a fusing of the bones in the spine. He also had arthritis in his elbows. His pain was managed with the help of medications. Panzer still adored Ruby and they were often together. Ruby loved to slam into Panzer, knocking him over. She was a tough dog and Panzer did not mind her idea of play. I would find them laying next to each other with their arms crossed in the same way. They were an adorable pair.

Cowboy also had spondylosis which created a pronounced hump in his back. Certain movements were painful for him. Many times, Cowboy would hide behind me or in my vegetable garden so Moose could not get to him. He loved wrestling and playing with Moose but his back was too rigid and painful.

Moose showed no signs of having any health issues other than fatty lumps.

Living on acreage was a blessing. There was lots of land for the dogs to run, get exercise and relieve themselves. I didn't take the crew on walks since they had plenty of room to run. The river access was close but if the sun was out it was usually occupied by people and sometimes dogs. One bright, rain free spring weekday, I talked Richard into walking Panzer, Ruby and Moose to the river. The walk was too much for Cowboy so he stayed home.

We were lucky, no one else was at the river. When we got to the water, Panzer and Ruby ran right in. They would swim down the river if I let them. I threw sticks in the river for Ruby and Panzer. They would excitedly race each other to the stick, sometimes bringing the stick back together.

Moose would wade knee deep into the water. That was his limit. He did not like getting water up to his belly. As a rule, Labradors love to swim, but not this one. Moose never seemed to mind baths however a full body immersion was off the table.

Moose watched Panzer and Ruby repeatedly chase sticks. Then much to my surprise, Moose walked straight into the water, neck deep and swam after the stick. He tried repeated to beat Panzer and Ruby to the stick. Once in a while he beat the champion swimmers and came back with the prize. I could not believe Moose was swimming like a true Labrador and enjoying it.

I've never experienced anything as beautiful as the Pacific Northwest in the summer. The skies a brilliant blue, trees are deep emerald green, the temperature and humidity are moderate, the air is clean. Everything sparkles like it's new.

Maintaining acreage means working outside every weekend in the spring and summer. The dogs stayed in their kennels during the week while I was at work. I tried making up for it on the weekends by spending time outside. I worked in the yard while the crew lounged around or patrolled the property. Moose would hunt, Panzer would lay in the shade, Ruby would harass Panzer and Cowboy would lay in the direct sun as long as he could stand it.

Moose loved helping me in the yard and would get excited when I would head towards the garden shed. He would trot beside me, excitedly looking up at me. When I came out of the shed with my tools, he would eye the long handled ones with expectation. I thought he might want to grab the tools in his mouth. I gave him the tool by the end next to the metal head. Thus he could balance the tool in his mouth as he carried it. He did so with pride. Running ahead of me, head and tail high in the air. I would direct him to where I needed him to go and tell him what a good helper he was. He dropped the tool where I need it then trotted off to finish his to-do list.

One night about 1 AM, Moose woke me, letting me know he needed to go out. I got out of bed, let him out and pulled the cover off the dog door. I had to get up in three hours for work so I went back to bed. When he came back into the house I would hear the flap of the dog door. I fell asleep waking an hour later when Moose jumped up on the bed. I got up to put the cover back on the dog door. Walking out of my room, I stepped on something wet. I thought one of the dogs had vomited even though I had not heard any of them get sick. I turned on the light and almost jumped out of my skin. I had not stepped in vomit - but wished I had. I stepped on a large rat Moose killed and brought in for me. Moose panted and watched me discover his gift. I thanked him and cleaned up his prize.

Back in Texas, my mother was doing well in the home she was in. I received frequent updates from her caretaker. She was a blessing. She and her husband doted on my mother, fed her, cared for her and catered to her needs. I did not get any complaints from my mother about her care. She patiently waited for my father to take her home. She recognized me less and less as she slipped deeper into her dementia.

Richard became scarce at the house. He was working several miles from the house and stayed with a friend during the week. He would stop in on the weekends picking up more clothes or visiting family but that was the extent of his time at the house.

Angela's cancer spread to other organs and she was forced back on chemo. I've never seen someone fight so hard and maintain such a positive attitude. Her drive to live came from not wanting to leave her animals which she loved more than anything else. I rarely asked Angela for help with the pack. She had enough on her plate. When I did need her, she happily fed my dogs and took care of their needs.

Life is ever changing and I tried to keep up with the adjustments. I was about to find out how well I could adapt.

CHAPTER 19

Learning My Limitations

Another year passed and changes in the dogs were more noticeable. Moose no longer jumped up on my bed. He would place his front paws on the bed, wag his tail and wait for me to lift up his back end. Cowboy didn't want to play with Moose anymore due to his back pain. His disposition remained sweet as ever. Panzer and Ruby - ever in love with each other - were also showing decreasing mobility.

February in the Pacific Northwest is usually winter's last blast and we got lots of snow. Snow invigorates Moose. All the dogs loved to play in the snow, but for Moose it was special. He ran, no, zoomed around the yard and invited Cowboy to wrestle. Cowboy would run and hide behind me to avoid playing with Moose. Moose's joy was infectious.

On March 26th, I got the phone call I expected for a long time. My mother's caretaker said my mother was transitioning and she didn't think she had long. If you have elderly parents, you know this call comes several times. Many times it's a false alarm. Then the one time - it isn't. Something told me her caretaker was not wrong.

I started making plans to get back home. I coordinated with Angela to take care of the dogs. I had to get their necessities together, contact my boss and more. I was searching the airlines for a ticket, I got another phone call. My mother's caretaker called to tell me my mother passed. It was only a matter of hours from the first phone call. Now I was forced to make different arrangements.

My mother's passing was not a surprise but heartbreaking nonetheless. I prayed for peace for her but was not prepared for the fallout of her passing. It's a somber, empty feeling knowing I had run out of family. Regardless of the kind of relationship you had with your family, when you are out of time, guilt and sadness become unavoidable.

I chose not to take any time off of work. I couldn't stand the thought of being alone in my house. I feared facing my emotions, the isolation and being vulnerable. My dogs were my comfort but I was alone. I felt it, heard it, lived it. It was harder than I thought it would be. I was failing to keep my head above water. I was sinking.

Life was not done challenging me. About 11 PM on a work night in April, I was asleep in bed. Panzer, Moose and Cowboy were sleeping in their places. Ruby was sleeping on the floor next to me.

I heard Ruby drop on her bed next to me. A little while later I heard her panting excessively which she did often. The vet had told me she had a heart murmur and was likely in heart failure. When her panting did not subside, I turned the lights on to see what was going on. I found Ruby on the floor by Panzer's bed. She lying on her side, panting. I tried a couple of times to get her up but she fell over and could not hold herself up. Fear ran through me. I called the emergency vet who said to bring her in right away.

It was the middle of the night and I was unable to lift Ruby by myself. I called Angela whose husband Stan was working the late shift. She came over to help. We managed to load Ruby into my truck. I grabbed my purse and rushed off for the 20 mile trip to the emergency vet.

Two techs came to the truck and helped get Ruby into their

office. She was still panting and unable to hold herself upright.

I was sitting on the floor with Ruby when the vet came in to tell me she believed Ruby's inner ear had ruptured. She said it was common in older dogs and Ruby would not recover. Ruby would not be able to stand or walk on her own anymore. She would have to be carried. The vet said if Ruby did show any improvement it wouldn't last long, only prolonging her suffering. I knew what I had to do. The vet gave her a sedative, she stopped panting, laid her head down and closed her eyes... forever. My beautiful princess was gone. It broke not only my heart but Panzer's too.

I went to pay and realized I did not have my wallet with me. During the work week, I put my wallet in my work bag. On the weekend it went back in my regular purse. In my rush to get Ruby to the hospital, I grabbed my weekend bag. I had no way to pay the bill. I called Angela and asked her to go to my house and get my wallet out of my bag.

As I drove home tears poured from my eyes for Ruby and Panzer. I wondered how Panzer would adjust. Ruby was free of pain and was in a better place. An orange light came on my dash. Then as par for the night, a warning - I was driving on my reserve tank of gas. Another over sight on my part. I felt defeated.

I drove home crying for the loss of Ruby. I wondered how Panzer would adjust. Ruby was free of her pain and she was in a better place. An orange light came on my dash. A warning light - telling me I was driving on my reserve tank of gas. Another over sight on my part. I had left my truck parked with very little gas.

I called Angela again and asked her to meet me with my debit card at a gas station close to our house. She told me Stan would meet me there. I pulled into the station and parked at the pump. Stan pulled in front of me. He got out of his truck pulling a crumpled $10 bill out of his pocket. I lost any composure I had left. He had gotten out of bed in the middle of the night and handed me his last $10 and a hug.

I went home and headed to my bedroom where the dogs were

still sleeping. Panzer stared at me as I crawled back into bed. He didn't know what had happened and I had no way of telling him. It wouldn't take long for him to understand his girl was gone.

Over the course of five years, I lost my family and two of my pack. My circle was getting smaller. I sunk deeper into depression and had difficulty finding the drive to do much.

I went to work later that morning. I had to. Working my profession teaches you to compartmentalize your emotions. I was afraid of being home alone with my emotions. Since they were eating at me from the place I was hiding them, I didn't want to know what they were capable of doing if I faced them. I started the slide into anxiety, deeper depression, exhaustion and hopelessness.

Anyone who has dealt with grief knows it comes in waves. When I experience something traumatic, I usually dive deep into the emotion. It helps me move on quicker. I had not done this. Instead I ran away from my emotions - hoping I could avoid them.

It was time to face my emotions and heal. My phobia of dying grew worse. I was afraid of losing my job or getting hurt because my head was in the wrong place. I found a great professional who helped me work through my emotions.

There were however good days in the mix, and most of them were thanks to my dogs. Moose continued to amuse me with his antics. He loves playing 'keep away' with me. He would get me to throw him a disc until I gave up, tossing him both discs. He would keep them in his mouth, walk towards me then turn his head and walk away as soon as I reached for them. He looked like he had duck lips when he held the two disc back to back.

One bright, sunny spring day, I went out the gate to get the mail. It's a short walk on a private road to the mailbox. Open approaching the side of the road I saw a cottontail that appeared to have been hit by a car. I grabbed my mail and headed back to the gate.

Cowboy hated when I went out of the gate and didn't take him. He would use his forepaws pulling the gate wide enough to squeeze through. I saw Cowboy in the field. He had pulled the gate open, escaping. Cowboy had the dead rabbit in his mouth. He didn't try to eat it. He laid there with the rabbit draped in his mouth. He looked as proud as if he had caught the rabbit himself.

I couldn't let Cowboy take his prize back on the property - there would be a fight over the rabbit. Cowboy refused to drop his prize. I didn't want to see that rabbit become a rope toy even if it was dead. I waited with Cowboy, petted him and told him what a good boy he was. In time, he released his catch and we went back home.

A few days later a friend from work came to visit. She had recently moved to the area and loved to explore so we chanced taking Moose to the river. We walked to the river and did not see any cars or people. There was a clearing on the river bank and we sat there. I let go of Moose's leash, leaving it attached in case I needed to grab him quickly.

While we sat and talked I threw sticks for Moose. He would swim into the river to get the sticks. I couldn't believe he was swimming again. When his feet were able to touch the bottom of the river, he would grab his leash in his mouth and walk out of the river. My friend found this very amusing. She thought he looked like he was walking himself. He was my boy, always full of surprises, comic relief and endearing moments.

The summer was typically beautiful with clear skies and moderate heat. The dogs and I spent most of our time outside well into the fall. I was slowly starting to come around. I was not in a deep depression, but I was not completely OK either. I was adjusting to the loneliness and the losses.

CHAPTER 20

Breathing Room

The next year gave me a chance to catch my breath. January 5th was my day off and I agreed to meet my friends Brad and Miguel for lunch at a restaurant near a municipal airport. The three of us knew each other from working in the same profession.

Miguel and I were still working but Brad had retired. Miguel is one of the hardest working people I know. He is smart, articulate and his kind demeanor solicited many confessions. I learned a lot working with him. Miguel also knows how to make the most of his time off. We would often get together for lunch on our days off. He was always cheerful and easy to be around.

Brad retired the year prior. He still talked about the 'good old days' when he was working. He was also cheerful and made friends where ever he went. Brad was doing odd jobs and one of them was helping his friend Michael work on planes. Brad had been working with Michael and brought him along. They arrived first at the crowded restaurant and sat in a booth across from each other. Miguel and I arrived at the same time. I spotted Brad and sat next to him. Miguel sat next to Michael.

Michael was tall, in his middle years and had dark,

greying hair. His eyes were a deep blue and his smile was infectious. He was confident and made conversation with all of us. After lunch, Michael asked us if we wanted to see the jet he was working on. We agreed. Miguel was curious and enjoyed learning about the jet.

A couple of weeks later Brad invited me to meet him and Michael in town for a drink. Brad mentioned he was going with a group of friends to a winter festival in the central part of the state and is a favorite summer tourist destination. The town is on a lake surrounded by foothills. I had never been there but heard it was beautiful. Brad asked me if I wanted to go. It had been a long time since I'd gone anywhere or done anything for myself so I agreed. Besides, Michael was going as well. I was only going to be gone a couple of days so I asked Angela to take care of my dogs. She cheerfully agreed.

Michael and I drove together and he brought his two dogs along. Chico was the size of a chihuahua but with long blonde hair and a curled tail. I later told Michael about the DNA tests for dogs and it revealed Chico was a Pomeranian and Chihuahua mix. Nico was medium sized, had short red hair and resembled a miniature Vizsla. The test revealed he was a Whippet and Chihuahua mix.

Michael and I talked about a lot subjects on the three hour drive. We learned a lot about each other. We arrived after dark in the small town which had a few inches of snow on the ground. The next day we bundled up and walked through the downtown area where the festival had been set up. It was set up like a street fair but with fires in various locations so you could warm up. There were booths lining the middle of the street with boutiques or activities for families. The stores and restaurants were open as well. It was a unique festival and I was glad I went.

Sunday afternoon we drove back to our side of the state. Our relationship began and grew. We were on the same page about most things in life. It was easy and seamless - like old friends from another lifetime. After a contemptuous relationship with Richard, this seemed like it was too easy and too good to be true.

Chico and Nico were friendly but they had no training. They didn't even know basic commands like sit or stay so I began basic training with them. Nico was food motivated and learned fast. Chico was stubborn and resistant. When he got frustrated he would try to bite. Michael had to work with him quite a bit before he decided he would comply with training.

When March arrived Cowboy was struggling to get around. There were times he wouldn't eat - this is never a good sign with an aging dog. I was confused the first time Cowboy did not greet me when I got home from work. He was always the first to greet me with a wagging back end. I found him inside the house lying down, looking towards the door for me. He looked almost apologetic with his ears pulled down and his tail flapping. It was crushing.

With each passing day Cowboy lost a little more mobility. Michael and I took him to see the vet Michael used who also administered alternative healing methods. The vet was a man of average build in his sixties. He had a round face, wore glasses and had a gentle disposition. He told us Cowboy's issue was likely a bone spur that came loose in his spine and was causing some paralysis. We tried acupuncture and herbal remedies. Nothing seemed to work.

A week later, we took Cowboy back to the vet. The vet told us this condition was common in dogs but he had not seen a case progress so fast. He assured me Cowboy was not in pain. That gave me some time to come to terms with what was happening.

Cowboy spent most of his time lying down. He loved laying in the sun and on sunny days we would put his cot on the deck. With Moose locked inside, we brought Michael's dogs to meet Cowboy. Cowboy loved meeting other dogs. Nico sniffed Cowboy and then went on his way. Chico walked up to Cowboy and licked his face. Cowboy perked up and if a dog could smile, he smiled. There are those that don't believe animals have emotions. If they could have seen the change in Cowboy's disposition they would be believers. The memory of seeing Cowboy enjoy Chico's company is one of my favorites.

On March 26th, exactly one year after the passing of my mother, we took Cowboy to the vet hoping for a miracle - there were no miracles to be had. The vet told us Cowboy's quality of life was severely diminished. He asked me a simple question. "Are you ready?" I broke down sobbing and said I would never be ready. The vet patted me on the back and comforted me the best he could. I hated having to make this decision. There is so much guilt associated with ending another's life. But I wasn't going to let my sweet boy suffer because of my weakness. I loved him too much.

I agreed it was time to let him go. Cowboy was lying on the floor panting. I wanted to release him from his prison. He was a joy to so many for so long. I owed him. I laid on the floor with my hand over Cowboy's heart. I sobbed into his fur while the vet administered the drugs. He took a sharp inhale and he was gone. I laid with him until the vet said he was gone and then I still waited. I have heard that consciousness persists for moments after death. I don't know how anyone would know that. But in case it was true, I held him a bit longer.

When I told Richard Cowboy was gone, his heart broke. The big goofy, sweet boy could worm his way into the hardest of hearts. Moose missed Cowboy. He lost both of his best pals from the pack. He no longer had a playmate, a friend to lie in the sun with or ears to clean. Cowboy left a hole in many hearts.

Michael moved into my house which created a challenge because of Nico and Chico. When people meet Moose they have a hard time believing he does not like animals. Michael was one of those people. What he and others saw was a dog that ran up to greet visitors, took treats with a soft mouth and a goofy dog that loved to play. Michael believed if we worked with Tommy, Moose would come around.

I knew better. I trusted Tommy so agreed to go through some training sessions. Tommy showed us some techniques to try that also kept the dogs safe. He explained it would take a long time for Moose to accept having these dogs in the house. The training was very stressful for Nico so I told Michael it was not worth it. I was also concerned about the size difference between the dogs. Moose was a powerful 100 pound dog. Nico and Chico were a fraction of his size. I was able to convince Michael he needed to accept Moose's disposition.

We needed to find a way to keep the boys safe while giving them a fulfilling life. We converted the outdoor kennel into a fortress. It was where my pack spent their days lounging while I was at work. The kennel was now going to be a luxury home for Nico and Chico.

We fully enclosed and insulated the kennel. Four windows were added where the stalls had been. The name plaques Stan had made for Cowboy, Moose, Panzer and Ruby were on the walls above the windows. It would always be their kennel. Next to the back door, we added a dog door on an automatic timer.

We fenced in a large area out the back door and one side of the kennel. The boys could use the dog door as needed to play or relieve themselves. We poured a two foot deep curb under the fence to deter digging. The welded wire fencing had quarter inch holes so teeth could not be used to pull on the fence. Boards were attached on both sides of the fence mid-height so the fence could not be pushed loose. We ran invisible fencing around the perimeter to keep Moose from coming within ten feet of the kennel.

Before we finished the construction, I asked Tommy to come over to see if he had any other suggestions. He suggested extending the fence to create an enclosed area around the front door. It was another safety measure in case the door was accidentally left open or if the boys got out of the door.

No luxury hotel is complete with out amenities. We put in a sink with an instant hot water tap, a small refrigerator, TV, couch and a heating and air conditioning unit.

Nico and Chico used the doggie door frequently. They would lounge in the grass, or bark at passerby's. We did not let Moose go outside on his own for quite some time. We watched him to see how he would react to seeing Nico and Chico in the kennel. In the beginning, Moose was not happy there were dogs on his property. A few times he tried to rush the fence. We stopped him and redirected him.

We asked Tommy to show us how to desensitize Moose to the presence of Chico and Nico. One afternoon, I came home from work and Michael had already begun working with Tommy. The gate to the driveway was open. Moose was lying in the grass near Michael and Tommy. Nico and Chico were in their fenced yard. All humans and canines were calm and safe.

Tommy was showing Michael how to keep Moose's attention focused on him. Michael learned how powerful Moose is. Earlier, Moose had charged the fence where Chico had been standing. He hit the fence hard. The invisible fence shocked Moose and he did not approach the fence again. Over time Nico and Chico were able to be out in the fenced area and Moose would ignore them.

As I got to know Nico better I found that he shares many traits with Moose. He is a fun, athletic dog. He loves to jump, runs sprints around the yard, tossing sticks in the air and tussling with Chico. He is very dog selective. He is also a great hunter - no mole, mouse, or bird is safe if Nico is in the area.

One afternoon we were sitting on the back deck having a BBQ with friends and family. Moose was outside and had been digging in the flower bed next to the back deck stairs. After several minutes I could hear Moose panting and continuing to dig. I got up to make sure he wasn't over doing it - I saw carnage. In one hole next to a tree, Moose had unearthed and killed two field mice, two moles and a weasel.

Michael and I had a system for letting the boys out in the yard. When Moose went out, Nico and Chico were in the kennel. When it was the boys turn to go out, we locked Moose in the house. Every door was locked, cross checked and the blinds were shut. Then it was safe to let Nico and Chico in the yard. Panzer could be outside with Nico and Chico. Chico would charge up to Panzer and lick his face. Panzer would bark and back away. Then he would follow Chico around seeking his attention.

Several years prior, I bought a bone shaped pool for the crew. Panzer still loved the pool and would use it often. Moose thought of it as a giant water bowl. Chico enjoyed swimming but had to be helped into the pool. Nico hated any kind of water. He would pancake when we said the word 'bath' or 'swim'. If we walked up to him he would cling to the ground then roll over exposing his belly.

Several years prior, I bought a bone shaped pool for the crew. Panzer still loved the pool and would use it often. Moose thought of it as a giant water bowl. Chico enjoyed swimming but had to be helped into the pool. Nico hated any kind of water. He would pancake when we said the word 'bath' or 'swim'. If we walked up to him he would cling to the ground then roll over exposing his belly.

January 5th, 2019 was the anniversary of the date I met Michael. We decided to go to dinner at one of our favorite restaurants at a port in a nearby city. The building has windows around the perimeter that face the water. We were early and Michael suggested we take a walk on the pier. We walked out to a part of the pier where there were no other people. Michael surprised me by getting down on one knee and proposing. He was so nervous he almost dropped the ring into ocean. I agreed.

I was happy but I found my self wondering when it would end. It seemed the pattern of my life was short lived happiness. I did not trust the happiness would last.

Michael and I planned on marrying in July. A week before the ceremony Stan came to my door to ask me if he could walk me down the aisle. He told me he thought of me as a daughter and it was his honor to stand in for me. He was crying and his hands shook. I couldn't say no.

Angela pulled me aside before the ceremony. She gave me the speech the mother in the movie Moonstruck gave her daughter. She had waited all her life to give that speech to her daughter who never married. Moose, Stan and Angela walked with me to join Michael under my favorite willow tree.

As the year went on, Panzer lost muscle mass and had more trouble getting around. Michael built a ramp to make getting in and out of the house easier but Panzer still struggled. If he would slip and fall, it was hard to help him get up without hurting him. He was becoming incontinent as well.

On the last day of the year, we scheduled a vet to come to the house to relive Panzer from his pain. I cried so many days leading up to this day. I hated to end his life. He loved life and made sure I knew it. He sought my attention all the time. Elderly dogs are so sweet. Yet, his immense pain was showing through his will to live.

A kind elderly woman vet came to the house. She had been a vet for a long time. She was patient and empathetic. Panzer settled down on his bed at the foot of our bed.

We spent time with Panzer, petting him and comforting him as the vet set up her medications. I placed Ruby's ashes next to him. Panzer sniffed, then licked the box. When the vet was ready, we shut the door so Moose could not come in. We did not want Moose's antics to cause stress for Panzer. Moose was already sniffing around the vet's bags looking for something to steal to get her attention.

When the vet put the needle in Panzer's arm he flinched. She told us that indicated Panzer was in a great deal more pain than he was letting on. It was a small comfort to me that I was making the right decision by releasing him of his pain. As Panzer relaxed he laid his head down on a stuffed lion that was next to his bed. He passed peacefully and surrounded by love.

Once we were sure Panzer was gone we let Moose in the room so he could see Panzer was gone. Moose crept up to Panzer and snatched the stuffed lion from under his head. We all laughed. Moose always knew when a situation needed lightening.

CHAPTER 21

The World Comes To A Screeching Halt

January 2020 came around and the world had no idea what was about to hit. Patient zero who brought Covid-19 to the United States lived in the same county I lived in and served. The world was just starting to panic. Lives would change forever from a virus. The impacts of Covid-19 were only getting started. In the beginning of the year, life was much the same as it had always been.

Moose was now going on eleven years of age. He was becoming more afraid of severe weather. This was a change from the dog that feared nothing. Strong winds and thunder now terrified him. I bought him a shirt to help with his anxiety. It seemed to work well. Nico and Chico were thriving in their new lives. We were hyper careful and had not had any accidental meetings between the trio.

In March I was told to work from home as much as I could - I did not enjoy working from home. A lot of work is social. I enjoyed meeting with my coworkers and bantering with them. I had planned to retire by July but I decided to retire early in April. It was a good decision as the world was now beginning to shut down.

The timing was a blessing for Moose and I. We spent most days together with a few exceptions. We fell into a routine of getting up together. Moose napped while I caught up on the world events. We would spend as much time outdoors as we could together. Moose would bark, groan and pace around if I spent too much time inside on a nice day. It was his way of asking me to stop what I was doing and enjoy the day with him. So we did.

We spent lots of time exploring and making up for the eleven years of his life that I worked full time. I imagine this is the ideal life for a dog, getting to spend every day, all day, with their beloved human. I know it has been for me as well. Being able to retire and enjoy the time with my senior best friend was a blessing.

I had no idea how much stress I was under from my job for the past twenty years. Coming down from it was a process and a slow one at that. I started walking almost daily. It was very therapeutic. I saw so much wildlife and habitat I had never seen before. Losing myself in the beauty of nature helped me realize there was more to life than death and despair. Adapting to retirement would be as challenging as it was enjoyable.

Moose's face was now more white than black. His lumps were multiplying and he had an occasional limp. I could feel lumps behind his ears, on his belly and even in his groin area. His age was starting to show but he seemed healthy. Moose loved having me at home and followed me everywhere. I felt privileged to be able to spend so much time with him in his senior years.

Dogs were being adopted in record numbers as most people were working from home. The world hoped and believed this pandemic would be over by the end of the year. It wasn't.

January 2021 was Moose's annual check up. He was going to be twelve soon. He started to moan when I petted him. He loved rub downs and the attention he got for making noise. There was a growth on Moose's muzzle that looked like a large skin tag and a round growth on his tongue. Moose's bloodwork showed him to be healthy with no major issues.

Michael and I took a road trip in March to Arizona for business. We decided to take Moose with us. The first day was rough for Moose. He was afraid of the noises the motorhome made. It was quite a bit louder and a bumpier ride than any truck Moose had ever been in. I sat with him and opened a window. The smells interested him and distracted him from his worries. By mid day he was getting less anxious. The second day he was a completely comfortable with riding in the motorhome.

Once we got to the house we were staying in, Moose was apprehensive but settled in quicker than I expected. He made his place on the couch where he took most of his naps. He enjoyed checking out this new environment but was not a fan of the prickly grass. Rolling in the grass and stretching out on the cool Washington grass was one of his favorite things. On the trip back I was able to drive my truck. We gave Moose the option of riding back home in the truck. He chose the motorhome with the couch.

A few weeks before Moose's twelfth birthday I had a vivid dream. I was holding an elderly Moose. I was crying and begging God for more time with him. I woke with a broken heart. In making that request - I knew I had to do my part if I was to get more time. I had to live in the moment, savoring the time I had without worrying when it would end. That would be a challenge for me.

Childhood friends of mine invited me and Michael to join them in Texas for a vacation. It had been years since I had been on a vacation or seen my friends. July promised to be hot and humid in Texas but I looked forward to the trip.

It was getting harder to find someone who could watch the dogs. Angela was still fighting cancer and having a hard time. She fought for her life while maintain her spunk and drive. Angela agreed to come over and feed the dogs in the morning. Stan would come over for mid day breaks and to spend the night with Moose.

The night before the trip I was having severe anxiety about leaving home. I wanted any reason not to go. It's a dramatic reaction but I could not put my finger on what was causing the anxiety. I had a strong feeling something bad was going to happen.

The next afternoon we landed in Texas. Angela had asked me to call her as soon as we landed. I called while we were waited for our bags. After a brief chat, she told me Stan needed to talk to me. Stan got on the phone and told me there was an incident with Moose and Chico. He told me Moose had gotten out the back door which he must not have locked. He was with Nico and Chico when Moose bit Chico twice on the back. He and Angel had rushed Chico to a vet and they needed me to call them.

Because of Covid a lot of vets were unable to make time to help Chico. Angela called emergency vets and they said their waits were hours long. They put Chico in their truck and drove into town. The hospital they chose was relatively new. Angela felt it would be harder for a vet to say no if they saw the condition Chico was in. Stan walked in to the hospital holding Chico, sobbing and begging for help. The kind hearted receptionist could not turn him away.

When I told Michael what had happened, he was angry, scared and sad all at the same time. I called the clinic and spoke with the receptionist. She explained there was a shortage of vets and most places were turning people and their pets away. They felt sorry for Chico and Stan and chose to help them. I was grateful they made an exception. Chico was stable and charmed the staff at the Vet's offie. He was going to need surgery to install drain tubes where Moose had bit him. His recovery was uncertain and it would take some time.

I told Michael I understood if he was mad at Moose. I didn't approve of Moose's behavior but his instincts could not be changed. I asked Michael to go easy on Stan as he was very upset. Michael was not mad at Moose or Stan, just worried about Chico. When we called Stan he was tearful and told Michael he was distressed about what had happened. He could not forgive himself. We asked him to be very carful with his safety procedures until we returned. Stan insisted on paying for Chico's surgery. It was quite a stretch for their budget but he would not let me argue with him.

The vet stayed late and took care of Chico. When a dog bites, they can tear the skin away from the muscle, causing the skin to die off. It looked like that was the case with Chico. The next day Chico was able to go home with pain medication and antibiotics. Stan and Angela set up an isolation kennel for Chico. There could be no playing or roughhousing between him and Nico.

When we got home I told Michael I was not going on any more vacations. Few people can manage dogs that cannot intermingle on the same property. It requires a great deal of diligence.

Chico ended up losing the skin on his back. We had to do bandage changes daily. He wore baby onesies over his bandage and a cone around his neck. He despised having to wear the cone. His skin healed well due to remarkable care from the vet. In a few weeks Chico was outside running around, playing with Nico, and rolling in the grass.

CHAPTER 22

Loving a Senior Moose

The new year rolled around and Moose was well on his way to his thirteenth birthday. He was now a year past the average life span of a Labrador. What I didn't know was how fast he would change. His personality became sweeter and much easier to manage.

Moose is always teaching me something new about life. He notices tiny details that often escape my attention. He seems to have an innate awareness of his surroundings that I can only aspire to. His enthusiasm for life is contagious.

In the afternoons, we would go for a walk around the yard. Moose takes his time to sniff and explore all the places he visited the day before. A typical walk involves munching on fresh grass, rolling around in the grass until it feels good against his fur, barking at people walking by, warning animals to stay away, searching for rabbit nests, checking mole holes, marking spots marked by the other dogs...the list goes on.

Every now and then he would look back at me. I wasn't sure if he was checking to see if I was still following him or if I was paying attention. We took these walks most days - weather permitting. We walked until he got tired or he had gathered all the information he needed.

One frosty morning, Moose and I went out to feed chickens. I walked down the stairs by taking one stair at a time. I turned around to see what Moose was doing. He had been paying close attention - he watched - then took one step at a time down the stairs. I put my hand on his neck so he could feel safer and I could grab him if I needed to. It fascinated me that he was aware of the slippery situation and determined how to proceed.

There were many changes in Moose but much stayed the same. Moose's attentiveness to me was one of his most endearing qualities. He still tried to grab my long handled garden tools. If I brought a small package from the mailbox, Moose would stare at it until I let him carry it back to the house for me.

Moose spent most of his days sitting on the couch, staring outside until he found something to bark about. If we were outside he would clear a spot under a bush, making a cool nest. From that spot he would take up watch. He searched for someone or something that needed a lecture on boundaries.

When Moose was younger, he would destroy a stuffed animal within minutes. An older, more mature Moose would do a little damage then carry his stuffy in his mouth for attention. If someone came to the house he would jump off the couch, grab his stuffy and run to greet his guest. He enjoyed the laughter, attention, and 'he's so cute' comments.

Many times I called Moose and saw him look around to try to find me. Moose seemed to hear well but had trouble sensing the direction of the sound. He had large fatty tumors below each ear that he loved for me to rub. Lipomas were all over his body and continued to multiply.

Moose's once all black face was now almost completely white. It made his whiskey brown eyes stand out. He had white on his chest, belly and paws. He also had a white strip from the underside of his tail to his belly.

For years Moose licked his left paw pad. After so much licking it became raw. The clinical name for this condition is lick granuloma. Lots of dogs will lick a lower limb until they make it raw. I had addressed causes ranging from allergies to behavior issues. Yet, he continued to lick the paw. I cleaned it and wrapped it on a daily basis. Moose tolerated my wraps for a while then he began tearing them off with his teeth.

The growth on his muzzle increased in size fast. It started to change in shape and consistency. I contacted his vet but he still did not feel it was necessary to remove the growth.

Another common ailment of elderly Labradors is laryngeal paralysis. The flap in the dog's throat becomes weakened and causes issues with drinking water. Moose would drink water then hack some of it back up. It is incurable. The condition also caused Moose to become more hoarse. His barks were low and deep.

When an older dog is quietly sleeping it makes your heart skip a beat. I would often hold my breath, watching him. I looked for the telltale sign of his chest rising and falling, the twitching of his paws or any other sign of life. I wondered if Moose's thirteenth birthday would be his last birthday.

At the same time, I wondered if this would be Angela's last year. Her cancer was taking over her body. I didn't know how much more her body could take. I ended up becoming her caretaker of sorts. I spent every evening with her, taking care of her needs. I learned a lot about her in those months. I also helped her get baptized. The same friend that married me and Michael performed this ceremony. It was quite touching to see the relief come over Angela when this was done. She wanted to be able to go to heaven and see her sister.

By May, the cancer took Angela's life. Angela fought hard to the very end. She passed a few weeks before Moose's birthday. Angela loved Moose almost as much as I did. Michael, Stan, her daughter and I were with her when she passed. As we watched her life slip away I saw a tear roll down her cheek. I wondered if this was a natural process or a conscious action. My belief is she knew her time was up and she was sad to leave us. I would miss her presence in our lives.

I rarely went anywhere without Moose. I was glad I didn't

have to work so I could spend every moment with him. Yet I often wondered if I could have done more - taken him out more - showed him the world more - gave him more hugs and kisses.

Moose's melanoma kept getting bigger. Every time it sloughed off its outer layer or grew, it would bleed. It got to the point where it was hanging below his upper lip. I took Moose to the vet, again. The Covid precautions had been lifted but I was not allowed to go in building with Moose. This caused him so much undue stress. The vet still did not think removal was wise for Moose.

A few weeks later, Moose's paw was so raw it was bleeding. I called the vet's office but didn't get a return call. I was not happy. The vet's assistant no longer answered incoming phone calls. She preferred to return calls at a later date, often days later. This was not the kind of care I wanted for either of us. It was sad to have to look for care elsewhere since this had been Moose's vet since he was months old.

A bleeding animal is an urgent matter so I tried the vet that took care of Chico's injuries. The tech felt the matter was urgent and scheduled me three weeks out. She promised to get him in right away if there was a cancellation. In the mean time I was able to wrap his paw and keep him from licking on it.

I did not have to wait long for a cancellation. A week later we were able to get Moose in to see the vet. The staff was friendly and accommodating to Moose's quirks. I brought a long hall runner to throw down on their tiled floors. Moose would not walk on hard floor, especially in areas new to him. They cleared the waiting area of animals so we could bring Moose into the room without incident. He took small, cautious steps on the carpet right into the room. Most importantly, I was allowed to go in the building and room with him.

The vet was a tall female with long blonde hair. She smiled when she walked in the room and greeted Moose. I told her all of Moose's conditions. She listened and then answered all my questions. I was sure she would take great care of Moose. This vet believed she could safely remove Moose's melanoma. She gave him a cone to keep him from licking his foot. Overall, Moose was in good shape and had the usual ailments a geriatric dog would have.

A week later, Moose's paw pad was still not healing. There was a large raw part which the thick, black covering was gone. There were parts of the pad that had spotty black patches which reminded me of melanoma.

I contacted the vet and sent her a picture. She decided Moose needed a biopsy of his pad. She moved his surgery up. Because Moose required anesthesia for the biopsy, the melanoma would be removed at the same time.

As Moose's surgery date neared I worried that Moose would not make it through the surgery due to his age and his laryngal paralysis. The vet was sure there would be no issues during the surgery. A tech called the night before with pre-op instructions. I held back tears and asked the tech to call me if it looked like Moose would not make it through surgery so I could be with him. I had a hard time controlling my emotions and my voice cracked. Saying it out loud made it a real possibility. The tech was empathetic and told me they would call me immediately if anything happened. It is kindness in times like this that makes people like her special. Showing compassion day in and day out is not easy for the average human.

The night before Moose's surgery, Cowboy came to me in a dream. He was his usual sweet, charming self. He laid next to me and put his head down for me to pet him. It was comforting to see him. I decided he had one of two messages for me. Either it would all be OK or he would love to be with Moose again. Which ever way it went. Moose was going to be in very good hands.

The following morning, I took Moose in for his appointment. I was tense and fearful but I tried not to communicate that to Moose. A tech came to help me get Moose out of the truck. When she opened the door to the office, the resident cat was sitting at the door. The tech got between the cat and Moose while the receptionist picked up the cat. Moose was nervous and sedated so he did not react to the cat.

We walked Moose down long hallways playing leap frog with mats and carpets stopping in the surgery center. The room had a large table in the center with secure kennels all around. There was music playing in the background. On one side of the room there was a door that led to a surgery room. There was a bright light on in the room and computer screens near the table. Opposite of that is the kennel where we placed Moose. The tech put some towels down on the concrete for him. I kissed him and told him I would be back for him. He laid down and stared out the kennel door. He crinkled his brow, his ears were up and his eyes focused. He was taking it all in.

Moose was the first one in surgery and he was done in one hour. The vet called told me the surgery was a success. I let out a breath I had been holding. She removed his melanoma from his muzzle leaving two stitches in it's place. A sample was taken from his paw pad leaving a hole which was closed with more stitches.

The following week, the vet called with the results of Moose's biopsy. She told the name of the condition causing his paw issues. It was a long name that did not end in 'noma. That meant he did not have cancer in his paw. I was ecstatic. The vet believed he had an immunity issue for which we would give him steroids. There were no visible scars on Moose's muzzle and no signs of the melanoma.

It's hard not to look at Moose without realizing he is on borrowed time. It's sad to think of a time I won't have his love in my life any longer. But, I made a promise I intend to keep. I will live in the moment and soak up every joy and ounce of love he gives me.

Moose's body slowly deteriorated but he was in good spirits. He tried to be the dog he once was. He would run to the fence barking at passing animals. His voice was becoming more and more hoarse. He would put on a good show but I could see he wasn't as fast as in his younger days. I worried less about his antics getting him in trouble.

Michael and I noticed Moose was limping again. We checked

his paw and saw the sore had opened back up. The following morning he was panting and salivating. He followed me around maintaining eye contact with me. I contacted the vet. She explained his paw had an autoimmune condition and was prone to flaring back up. He went on another round of steroids.

In December Moose had his semi-annual check up which showed his heart and lungs were in good condition. His liver enzymes were elevated due to his steroid use. The paw finally healed so we could wean him off the steroids. Overall, he was a healthy old man.

By the end of the year, Moose was no longer comfortable sleeping in my bed with me. One night when Michael was out of town, Moose and I were watching TV in bed. Moose started to pant and scratch at the covers. He wanted help getting down. I felt the full effect of Moose's aging. My heart broke and I started to cry. I looked right at Moose and spoke to him. I reminded him we had spent every day we could together and I couldn't believe he wanted to be on his own. He held my gaze while I cried and spoke to him. His raised his ears and his forehead creased. When I stopped talking, he got up and laid next to me stretched out against my leg. I was not ready for this change in our journey together.

The next night, I tucked Moose in on the couch. It was a sad sign of changing times but I wanted him to be comfortable - even if I was not ready to slowly start letting go.

CHAPTER 23

Shooting For Fourteen

Moose was now closing in on his fourteenth birthday. One day Michael and I were working around the house. Moose became anxious and could not find a comfortable spot to lay down. He would stand up and scratch the couch. I gave him the full dose of his prescribed pain killers. It did not seem to have much of an effect on him. Bed time came and I had to give him more medication.

The next two days he was his usual calm, happy self. I discussed his behavior with his vet. She prescribed a second medication which would help the pain killers work better. The vet was my calming beacon. She answered my questions and encouraged me to call if he did not improve. Her compassion and knowledgable demeanor kept me grounded.

I noticed Moose started drinking three to four bowls of water a day. The vet wanted to get a blood test to recheck Moose's liver values. The test showed his liver enzymes had dropped well within the normal range. He had been off the steroids for about a month which accounted for the decrease.

The next step was to get a urine sample. His symptoms resembled those of Cushing's syndrome. My research showed this occurs when a tumor grows on the pituitary or adrenal glands. The symptoms mimic those associated with aging dogs. The results of the urine test was also within normal values.

Moose's vet and I rehashed his symptoms. She told me he very likely has Canine Dissociative Disorder. This is similar to dementia in humans. I felt better knowing he did not have any crippling ailments.

I am OK with him having dementia. After all, I had been through that with my mother. I could do it again. It would break my heart to have Moose not recognize me. He was already seeking Michael more than me. But, he's with me, he's comfortable and we'll take this final battle on together.

God sent me my dogs at a time that we needed each other the most. He will let me know when to send Moose home. After every major loss in my life, Moose was there. I can not bear the thought of losing my best friend. It is his comforting, constant presence I will need after he passes.

My plan is to close the story here. I made you cry in the beginning and through the book I am sure. You and I have the same heart. We love dogs we have never even met. I know you will understand my pain when it is time to let my sweet boy go to be with his pack again. But I won't put you through that here. I want you to remember Moose for all the joy he brought to those who met him whether in person or on line.

❖ ❖ ❖

My dearest Moose,

Fourteen years ago, you called out to me from your jail cell. You were alone, scared, dirty, and infected with mange. I heeded your call with the intention of helping you and finding you a home. Fortunately that plan failed and you became a part of my pack. I had no idea you were my once in a lifetime dog, but you did. You were the last member in and the magic the pack needed.

I have to thank the man who tossed you out of his truck. I thank him for giving me the perfect dog. My heart believes he waited for someone to get behind him before he put you out on the street in a garbage bag.

I owe a a huge thank you to the lady who saw him do it. She thought she would find a baby in the bag. She could have left you in the street when she saw you were a puppy. Instead she did the right thing and took you to the local PD.

You looked at me like I was your hero. I did everything in my power to live up to that. You were not an easy dog. I cried many times over your antics and worried about how I would keep you safe and other animals safe from you. Though you didn't like other animals, you never met a human you didn't love.

When I needed a friend, you were there. When I needed to laugh, you did something silly. You showed me every day what is important. Love without conditions, do what you love, live in the moment, and make the best of every second. Life and love are beautiful gifts.

Thank you for being the constant in my life, for loving me and teaching me about love. You were my perfect dog. I can't wait to see you again my dear sweet boy. What a fantastic ride it has been. I will never stop loving you. Everything I did, I did for the love of Moose.

❖ ❖ ❖

> 1 Corinthians 13:4-8 Love is patient and kind; love does not envy or boast; it is not arrogant or rude. It does not insist on its own way; it is not irritable or resentful; it does not rejoice at wrongdoing, but rejoices with the truth. Love bears all things, believes all things, hopes all things, endures all things. Love never ends..

I should have named you Love.

FOR THE LOVE OF MOOSE

AFTERWORD

Our mentors, our catalysts, our teachers show up in our lives whether we are ready for them or not. We may not even realize we need them. If we are willing students, they challenge us, help us become better people, and teach us lessons about life and love.

Dogs give and teach unconditional love. Dogs don't care who they spend their lives with. They put up with offenses and mistakes and love us nonetheless. While humans don't put up with our shortcomings or uncleanliness, dogs don't take issue. They never care what their companions look like or smell like or what clothes they wear. As long as their person is kind and keeps them fed and free from harm, they're satisfied.

Dogs have the most basic of needs for food, security, and love. Unlike humans, dogs take many abuses and forgive, time and time again. Many dogs are abused, starved, beaten, and some are chained outside. Yet they come back to their abuser hoping for a gentle stroke, a loving look, or a kind word. Abused dogs may become timid and have scars on their hearts, but they forgive their abusers time and time again.

I am no better than any other human. I get angry. I can carry a grudge. I can be judgmental. I know how to love without conditions, but I don't do it often enough. How do we get back to our childhood state of loving without conditions? I don't know if we can. I try to forgive. Can I take a beating and forgive the hand that struck me? I'm not sure I can. Is it about living in the moment? Maybe. But how do you break down the scars and erase the memories? Humans commit unforgivable acts against one another. I'm not condoning or accepting abuse—physical or emotional. But forgiveness frees the victim from being chained to the abuser.

I have a difficult dog. My dog doesn't like other animals, but he's a good dog. He takes a lot of work and personality management. I recently learned of a support group for owners of difficult dogs in another state. I could put a group like that to good use. We are closeted owners. We fear people judging our dogs and calling them dangerous. But a dangerous dog is a difficult dog that is not managed.

Moose and I are deeply bonded to one another. From the day I pulled him out of that kennel—the same day someone threw him out of a truck in a garbage sack—we have had a special bond. I love Moose with my whole heart and soul, and I believe he loves me the same way. Wherever I go, Moose is my shadow.

Dogs hang on our every word, trying to understand what we want from them. Leaving them upsets them, and they listen for every sound that might reveal their beloved's return. They alert us to perceived dangers and run out into the blackest of night to protect us from unseen foes. They are our bravest and staunchest defenders. They are our dogs.

Whether a dog is blind, deaf, or has behavior problems, consider taking that angel under your wing. Those types of dogs take more work, but I promise you will not regret it. Special-needs dogs aren't for everybody, but neither a shelter nor the streets is a place for any dog. The challenges will be many with this kind of dog in your home. I had my share of challenges and shed many tears of frustration, fear, and love. I was sometimes scared to death Moose would be taken away from me—or worse, killed because he hurt another animal. It all made me stronger and helped me build better relationships.

Many times I was the teacher, but I was most often the student. If your eyes and heart are open, you stand to learn many lessons from a teacher that uses no words. My wish for you is to find your own once-in-a-lifetime dog.

ABOUT THE AUTHOR

Margaret Ludwig

About The Author

Margaret Ludwig (now Lee) was born in the great state of Texas. She moved to the Pacific Northwest in 1990 and loves it for all the area offers.

For the Love of Moose is her first book inspired by her love of dogs. Raising a pack of five dogs with strong personalities drove her to share what she learned about dogs and life itself. The original version published in 2016. This version brings the reader up to date.

Margaret loves gardening, exploring the outdoors, creative endeavors, spending time with her dogs, and reading.

She can by contacted through her website, www.fortheloveofmoose.com

FOR THE LOVE OF MOOSE

Made in United States
North Haven, CT
26 May 2023